Library of
Davidson College

HUMAN COMMUNICATION HANDBOOK
Simulations and Games
Volume 2

HUMAN COMMUNICATION HANDBOOK
Simulations and Games
Volume 2

Brent D. Ruben, Ph.D.
Rutgers University
New Jersey

HAYDEN BOOK COMPANY, INC.
Rochelle Park, New Jersey

For

Nate and Ruth Ruben — Parents and Friends

Library of Congress Cataloging in Publication Data

Ruben, Brent D
   Human communication handbook.

   Vol. 2 by B.D. Ruben.
   Includes bibliographies.
   1. Interpersonal relations. 2. Communication--
Social aspects. 3. Communication--Psychological
aspects. 4. Interpersonal communication--Problems,
exercises, etc. I. Budd, Richard W., joint author.
II. Title.
HM132.R82   301.14   74-23696
ISBN 0-8104-5765-2

Copyright © *1978 by HAYDEN BOOK COMPANY, INC.* All rights reserved. No part of this book may be reprinted, or reproduced, or utilized in any form or by any electronic, mechanical, or other means, now known or hereafter invented, including photocopying and recording, or in any information storage and retrieval system, without permission in writing from the Publisher.

Printed in the United States of America

1 2 3 4 5 6 7 8 9   PRINTING

78 79 80 81 82 83 84 85 86   YEAR

Preface

It is probably impossible to appropriately acknowledge all those persons whose ideas have been influential in the preparation of this book. First, the concept of this volume is an extension of *Human Communication Handbook: Simulations and Games, Vol. 1*. I am grateful to Dick Budd, co-author of that volume for his encouragement on this project, and his many intellectual contributions to my thinking about experiential learning.

Many of the games and exercises on intercultural communication grow out of my affiliation with the Canadian International Development Agency, Briefing Centre, during the course of the past five years. I am especially grateful to Dan Kealey of the Centre, who has been an important catalyst in my thinking about cross-cultural communication, in general, and a number of the activities on that topic presented in this book. I am also thankful to Pri Notowidigdo, Elizabeth Racicot, John Wallace, Chuck Pieper, Lanie Melamed, and Jennifer Fisher from whom I've learned a great deal. I am beholden also to Pierre Lortie, Director of the Briefing Centre for his support and encouragement.

Other inputs came in the area of intercultural communication as a result of my involvement with the Michigan State University-United States Agency for International Development Communication Seminars. During several years of active participation in that program I was fortunate to work with and learn from a number of outstanding individuals, especially Larry Sarbaugh and Bob Sallery, who then directed the program, and to whom I am indebted for the valuable experience the opportunity afforded.

With regard to the simulations and games in mass communication, a thankful nod to the work of Mal MacLean, Al Talbott, Lee Thayer, Dick Budd, Todd Hunt, and Gary Galinsky.

More generally, I also want to express my gratitude to those Rutgers students who with their provocative ideas provided further insight into communication education.

My sincere thanks to Bruce Kalter and Kathi Teichman for the help they rendered in the preparation of this manuscript, and to Dianne Littwin and Vijay Franklin of Hayden Book Company for their editorial assistance.

Finally, I'm grateful to my wife Jann, whose patience, interest, encouragement, and concern I've come to take for granted. Also, I want to thank my children, Robbi and Marc, who have taught me more about games than I've often cared to learn.

BRENT D. RUBEN

Credits

The author wishes to acknowledge the following contributors to *Human Communication Handbook: Simulations and Games, Vol. 2*.

Game 1: Adapted from an exercise developed by David Davidson and Brent D. Ruben, Rutgers University.

Game 2: Adapted from *The Memory Game*, developed by Robin Levit, Rutgers University.

Games 4, 8, 9, 10, 11, 12, 13, 22, and 25: Adapted from activities developed by Thomas E. Harris and Robert Smith, Wichita State University.

Games 5, 7, and 35: Adapted from activities developed for use at the Michigan State University-Agency for International Development Communication Seminars.

Game 14: Adapted from an activity developed by Robert J. Myers, Rutgers University.

Games 17 and 33: Adapted from activities developed by Lanie Melamed, McGill University, Montreal, Quebec.

Games 26, 27, and 32: Adapted from activities developed by the Briefing Centre, Canadian International Development Agency, Ottawa, Ontario.

Game 19: Developed by Nancy L. Harper, University of Iowa.

Game 28: Adapted from an exercise developed by Raymond Rouse for the Briefing Centre, Canadian International Development Agency, Ottawa, Ontario.

Game 29: Adapted from an exercise developed by Joan Wilson and Margaret Omar, Foreign Service Institute, Department of State, Washington, D.C.

Game 34: Adapted from a game developed by Cathy Bonner, Robin Levit, and Cheryl Saporowski, Rutgers University.

Game 36: Adapted from an exercise developed by Malcolm S. MacLean, Jr., Albert D. Talbott, University of Iowa, and Brent D. Ruben, Rutgers University.

Game 37: Adapted from an exercise developed by Richard W. Budd, Rutgers University.

Games 40 and 41: Adapted from activities developed by Todd Hunt, Rutgers University.

Contents

Prologue 1
Introduction 9
PART 1—Intrapersonal Communication 45
    1. Communication Inventory *48*
    2. Experience, Attention, and Memory *50*
    3. Assumptions, Context, and Expectations *52*
    4. Values and Decision-Making *53*
    5. Meaning and Category Formation *56*
    6. Perceptual Patterning *58*
    7. Language and Meaning *59*
    8. Message Set *61*
    9. Observation and Inference *63*
    10. Listening I *65*
    11. Listening II *66*
    12. Listening III *67*
    13. Listening IV *68*

PART 2—Social Communication 71
    14. Self-Concept and Self-Disclosure *74*
    15. Dyadic Communication *76*
    16. Non-verbal Cues and Stereotyping *78*
    17. Environment *81*
    18. Roles *82*
    19. Selective Perception, Debate, and Decision-Making *85*
    20. Organizational Roles: Leadership/Followership *87*
    21. Sex Role Perceptions *90*
    22. Values, Vocational Roles, and Group Decision-Making *93*
    23. Organizational Decision-Making *95*
    24. Organizational Dynamics *98*
    25. Values and Society *101*
    26. Culture I *103*

PART 3—Cross-Cultural and Intercultural Communication . .107
  27. Culture II *111*
  28. Culture III *113*
  29. Cross-Cultural Communication Guide *116*
  30. Cross-Cultural Effectiveness *122*
  31. Cultural Intervention *124*
  32. Inter-Racial, Intercultural, and International Values *126*
  33. Cross-Cultural Bargaining and Negotiation *130*
  34. Cross-Cultural Development Case Studies *134*
  35. Language and Cross-Cultural Communication *141*

PART 4—Mass Communication 147
  36. Biographical Interviewing *150*
  37. Interviewing and Perception *151*
  38. Written Communication *152*
  39. Perception, Levels of Analysis, and Context *154*
  40. Message Design and Style *156*
  41. Information Selection and Display *160*

PART 5—Communication Observation and Recording Guides 163
  1. Descriptions of Common Roles *166*
  2. Role Behavior Recording Form *168*
  3. Group Communication Observation Form *169*
  4. Recording Information Networks *171*
  5. Small Group Interaction Content Guide *172*
  6. Intra-Group Perception Guide *173*
  7. Verbal Interaction Recording Guide *175*
  8. Seating Arrangement Recording Guide *177*
  9. Interpersonal Communication Observation Form *179*
  10. Guideline for Providing Useful Feedback *180*
  11. Individual and Group Climate Guide *181*
  12. Empathy *182*
  13. Orientation to Knowledge *183*
  14. Role Behavior *184*
  15. Interaction Management *185*
  16. Interaction Posture *186*
  17. Respect *187*

HUMAN COMMUNICATION HANDBOOK
Simulations and Games
Volume 2

PROLOGUE

A Process Concept of Communication Education*

Malcolm S. MacLean, Jr.

With an appreciative nod to Harold Benjamin who wrote a magnificient little book called *The Sabre-Tooth Curriculum,* I will start off with a story. You will recognize it immediately as a fable of sorts.

Around the turn of the century at Midwestern University, then not nearly so huge as it is today, there was a young engineering professor named J. Worthington Peabody. Quite unusual among the engineering professors of his day, Peabody had actually worked in the real world for several years before he decided to return to the University, acquire a doctorate degree, and spend the rest of his life teaching the young how to be competent engineers. During that "working" period of his life, he had joined such eager young men as R. E. Olds and Henry Ford in tinkering with and developing our first automobiles.

Peabody was a serious scholar. (His book, *Applied Mechanics,* became a standard text in the field.) The students liked him, and one of the things they enjoyed most about Peabody was that he let them, even urged them to, join him in his favorite hobby—automobile building. Professor Peabody, these students felt, was concerned about *real* things, quite unlike some of their other professors.

Dr. R. P. Thunderbolt, Dean of Engineering, was not unaware of Peabody's popularity. In fact, he was rather fond of tinkering with the new machines himself. So, when, in the Spring of 1907, Peabody suggested a new course in the design and building of automobiles, Thunderbolt agreed immediately, pleased by the initiative of young Peabody. But, he warned the young man, in order for the course to pass the University's curriculum committee, they would have to give it a title and catalogue description which would emphasize its academic characteristics. They decided to call it: "Fundamental Principles of Automobilistic Engineering."

Two years later, at the convention of the Engineering Teachers Association, in a session on "New Developments in Engineering Education," Peabody proudly described the new course. Other teachers swarmed around him after the talk, wanting to know what textbook he was using and what kinds of laboratory exercises he considered most useful. Suffice it to say that, within three years, all but the most staid of the major schools had some kind of course in automobilistic engineering.

But Peabody and Midwestern did not stand still. One course could not possibly cover the rapidly expanding knowledge in the field. By 1912, Midwestern listed a full-fledged sequence in automobilistic engineering.

---

*An adaptation of a position paper prepared for the Educational Policies Committee, School of Journalism, University of Iowa, November, 1966.

Reactions varied; some of the other professors in engineering resented the popularity of the new sequence. They considered it too applied, too vocationally oriented. A few referred to it as "Peabody's Piddle!"

I hope I have not conveyed the impression that automobilism students took only vocational courses, for actually they took much of their work in liberal arts and general engineering. It was felt that the automobilist ought to be a broadly educated man. (Nearly all of them were men, since the industry managers generally refused to hire women in those days.)

One of these new courses, introduced in the fall of 1916 by a professor who had worked a summer in an airplane factory, dealt with principles of airplane design and manufacture. Students poured into this new course, hoping thus to prepare themselves for good jobs in this wildly growing industry. Professor Cartwright Boeing, the School's airplane man, urged Peabody to hire three more faculty members so they could field a full sequence in airplanism. Other faculty members fought acceptance of the new sequence until Boeing assured them that students electing it would be required to take the basics: Fundamentals of Auto Design I, Fundamentals of Auto Design II, Auto Body Manufacture, Auto Distribution and Sales and Auto Management. Professor Larke Studebaker convincingly argued that auto design, at least the way he taught it, was basic to the design of any kind of transportation equipment. "We should not be misled," he said, "by the glamour of this new industry."

Several of the auto manufacturers, when they heard of the new sequence, expressed their displeasure directly to Peabody and Hanley. They felt the new sequence might dilute the work in and draw good students away from automobilism. Peabody assured them that automobilism would always be central. Schools of Automobilism had sprung up and developed particularly in the large state universities. And many of the smaller colleges had at least a one-man department.

Several of the automobile and airplane manufacturing companies had grown quite large. Since the labor market was favorable for them, they usually hired their engineering and middle-management people from the high prestige eastern universities which, for some reason, had never developed schools of automobilism. Or these large firms took experienced men from the smaller ones. Since their top managers themselves had had general engineering and liberal arts when they were in college, they saw no need for the apprentice-like training that seemed to be going on in automobilism schools.

Well, you are probably quite aware of the more recent developments in this story, so I'll only remind you of some of the more important ones. For example, you'll recall the impact of the general education movement in higher education during the thirties and forties. While it provided some much-needed broadening for many university students, in some places it merely stimulated the development of what I like to call "smatterings" courses. In almost every department of the university you still find these today under titles starting with "Survey of . . ." or "Introduction to . . ."

Of course, there was the development of graduate studies, first leading to the masters degree. Now, in about two dozen schools, there is the Ph.D. in

Transportation Manufacturing Processes (in some places simply called Manufacturing Processes). Remember the big flap several years ago when Jack Tube argued that the "damned manufacturologists in the big schools with Ph.D. programs ought to go back home to the physics departments." He was particularly worried about the growing tendency in A schools to hire Ph.D.'s in "manufacturology" with little or no practical experience, instead of the "real pros" from the automobile business.

My fable has no end. It can't be true; nothing like that could actually happen, not in higher education related to automobile manufacture. Perhaps it is only a caricature of departments of mobile homes and schools of hotel and restaurant management.

In any case, I have told the fable to illustrate some of the benefits and dangers of modeling university curricula solely in terms of real world activities. In communication schools, we have a number of components: advertising, television production, film, magazine journalism, news-editorial journalism, persuasion, photojournalism, public relations, and radio. This situation probably helps to attract students who aspire to careers in newspapers, magazines, radio and television stations, advertising agencies, public relations, etc. It probably also helps to maintain good working relationships between the university and various industries or agencies.

But this set-up and the relationship of communication programs to other programs in the university have some serious drawbacks, I think. These may become clear as we look into objectives and relate these to some principles of learning and education. (For the latter, I have drawn on Jerome Bruner's *The Process of Education,* a talk by Gordon Lee on the revolution in education, Sir Geoffrey Vickers' *The Art of Judgment,* Abraham Kaplan's *The Conduct of Inquiry* and others.)

The general nature of the content of communication for many occupations is more or less given by the nature of the occupation. In the main, the lawyer communicates about law, the politician communicates about political issues, the minister communicates about God and man, etc. But there are also many jobs where the communicator is also a facilitator of communication among various elements of the system. He must be able to handle many kinds of content. He may act on behalf of his receivers, searching out and bringing them information, thus contributing to their well being and satisfaction. Or he may act on behalf of some sending source who pays him to help the source communicate to some set of receivers. Essentially he aids transactions among elements of a social system.

This communication type includes not only mass communicators—reporters, editors, photographers, in various media news organizations, the various people who create advertisements—but also many people within business and government who are responsible for maintaining adequate communication among elements in their own systems and between their systems and others.

As I look around at our graduates in their jobs, and as I observe today's communication professionals, I am impressed by several things. There are many things communication alumni do at almost every level of responsibility and authority. Sometimes, of course, there are hacks working in highly restricted jobs for unimaginative, dull employers, but invariably, I find keen, perceptive, and sensitive people in positions offering wide opportunities working for responsible and dedicated employers. Occasionally though, I wonder if we may not be training too many of the hacks. I know that typically we require our undergraduates to take roughly 75 percent of their work outside Schools of Communication and, in this sense, are more "liberal" than most other professional programs and some academic programs. I know too that some of our communication courses are generic. Yet I think we may have set our sights too low and allowed our powder to get wet. I don't mean by this that we must try to train every student to become a James Reston or a Leo Rosten or a Harry Reasoner. I'm sure we couldn't, even if we tried. But I do think that much more than we seem to be doing now, we must stretch our students' intellects, hone their skills of intuitive judgment and synthesis, give them tools for rigorous analysis of public problems, stimulate their creative thinking, build their love of learning and communicating—do these things and much more—so they will never be content with a hack job or dull employer. I simply don't believe that our society, in its dynamic movement, can stand hacks in key communication roles.

What are our objectives? What should they be?

We are trying to train people who can and will keep the members of our society truly well informed about matters of concern to them, particularly in their decisions as citizens in a democratic society.

We are trying to educate people who will later create or facilitate those kinds of communication necessary to the maintenance and improvement of our governmental, educational, business and other enterprises.

We are trying to educate people who will in turn help to achieve the above objectives through teaching and through scholarly and scientific research in communication.

One of our major jobs seems to be processing and distributing students for some often not well defined areas of the labor market. We have an obligation to these students, to their future employers and colleagues, to society generally and to ourselves to insure that our "processing" makes an important difference. We should *affect* these students in many ways. Here are some I consider most important:

—increased ability in the use of written and spoken language and other common message codes.

—solid grounding in those principles of communication which help to form a framework for continuing experimentation in strategies and tactics of communication.

—increased awareness of the historical growth and development of our major institutions, including our institutions of communication and enculturation.

—increased understanding of important similarities and differences among the peoples of the world generally in cultural matters as well as more specially in their styles and patterns of communication.

—fuller sense of the ways of science and art, not particularly of the special techniques but rather an understanding of what scientists and artists are about.

—greater familiarity with the laws, norms and standard operating procedures of the occupational areas they hope to enter and some knowledge of how these arose and how they relate to the central communication tasks.

—heightened creative imagination, inventiveness, and intuitive judgment along with the skill and courage to experiment.

—deeper concern with the process rather than merely the products of communication.

—stronger philosophical base in ethics, value, epistemology, that is, ways of thinking about and judging ethics, values, learning, etc.

—more intense love of inquiry, learning and communicating learning to others.

—greatly increased ability to analyze and synthesize.

Now, I want to discuss some implications I see in the above objectives. One overriding implication: We must become much more experimental ourselves in our whole education venture. We need the kind of intellectual environment in which both we and our students are encouraged to creative invention, to try different ways of teaching, of learning, of communicating. Along with this we need to develop some reasonable ways of continuously evaluating what we are doing.

We must find ways to help our students to go through such experiences that they will learn, learn to learn and learn to love learning and learn to love communicating learning to others. Among other things, we might translate Dewey's "learn by doing" into "learn by teaching" into "learn by communicating."

Let me give an example of something of this nature we might try. Many students have a hard time understanding and integrating the work they get in the great diversity of courses we require them to take. Furthermore, these courses in themselves usually give the students relatively little experience in communicating. Suppose we set up a course on courses. In this course X, we should have each student write, say, two papers (roughly five pages each) in which he would do his best to *communicate* to other students in the class how the work he is taking in another course relates to or helps in understanding some contemporary problem. At the same time he would be asked to read and evaluate the papers of, say, four other students. The primary job of the instructor would be to help his students develop useful frameworks for handling these tasks. He would sample the work done, the papers and their evaluation, mainly to see how well his students are learning. Something of this sort, I think, might help students to learn a lot more from their other courses, give them a good sense of the problems of communicating as well as valuable practice in doing so. Furthermore, it might feed some burning questions back to the instructors of the other courses, helping them to make their courses more relevant to the students' concerns.

The curriculum of a subject, Bruner says, should be determined by the most fundamental understanding that can be achieved of the underlying principles that give *structure* to that subject. Teaching specific topics or skills without making clear their context in the broader fundamental structure of a field of knowledge is uneconomical in several ways: 1) It makes it very hard for the student to generalize from things he meets now to those he meets later; 2) It provides little reward in terms of intellectual excitement, since the power to generalize helps make things worth knowing; 3) Knowledge without cohesive structure is easily forgotten.

For maximum learning in an area, we seem to need a continuous moving back and forth from the more abstract and general principles to the specifics, including practice. In the long run, this means a kind of spiraling up from the simple to the more complex, where we keep returning to fundamental principles and their practical implications at what would earlier have been more difficult levels.

Bruner points out that drill need not be rote and that too much emphasis on "understanding" (theory) may lead a student to an empty verbal glibness. Practice seems to be a necessary step toward understanding fundamental ideas. The point would be to get them reading and listening to a great diversity of styles, first for the fun of it, then to analyze how these styles relate to each other or differ in important characteristics, then to use them as models in writing and speaking.

We tend to limit our students' speaking and writing to the amount we can "grade." This seems to assume that students can't learn much without correction and that our correction does a lot of good. I doubt this, particularly when the corrections deal primarily with "wrong" grammar, gestures, spelling, punctuation and divergence from prescribed style. I wonder if we cannot find, or even develop ourselves, some self-instructional approaches to learning grammar, spelling and punctuation. In some settings, at least, these have worked better than blue pencils. And, as I suggested earlier, I wonder if we can't make good use of the students in a class as evaluators of each others' communications. They would get double benefits: 1) Rather direct and quick feedback from peers on how well they communicate, and 2) experience in an important kind of evaluation which in turn may suggest some new approaches in their own writing and speaking.

The teaching and learning of structure, rather than simply the mastery of techniques, Bruner says, is at the center of the classic problem of transfer. Supporting habits and skills make possible the active use of the materials one has come to understand.

The foundations of any subject may be taught to anybody at any age in some form. The basic ideas that lie at the heart of all science and mathematics or the basic themes that give form to life and literature are as simple as they are powerful.

Much too much, I think, we deal with conclusions from our field rather than with experimentation and inquiry. Can we help to train intuition, a most important factor in communication decisions? Bruner calls intuition the intellectual technique of arriving at plausible formulations without going through the analytic steps by which such formulations would be found to be valid or invalid conclusions. Can we help our students get the kinds of experiences which will lead them more often than not to sound hunches, shrewd guesses, fertile hypotheses, even give them the courage for an occasional leap to a tentative conclusion?

Is it possible at the same time to have them develop the tools and attitudes for analytic rigor which, in proper time, can bring the intuited idea into observation and close question? Further, how might they learn to synthesize, give form and make understandable a whole set of observations.

Again, I would like to suggest an idea which is not new except possibly in its emphasis: A form of the "great issues" kind of course. This would start with a detailed case problem in one of the areas vital to human welfare such as population control, human rights, automation, integration, etc. Then we might have relevant experts—say an economist, a historian, a systems engineer, a biologist, a psychologist, an anthropologist, etc.—take the "same" problem and demonstrate how they would analyze it, what kinds of data they would observe, what sources they would draw upon, etc. The students, we hope, would not merely observe passively, taking notes to be crammed for the next exam. Rather, they would write, discuss, or strive to persuade, search out illustrative materials, go to the library for more background material, interview the experts on matters they did not understand well, finally constructing "packages" intended to give particular receivers the kinds of experiences which would help them to understand the given problems. After a whole round of experts, the students would be challenged to synthesize what they had learned in terms of what some particular receivers might want and need to know about the problem.

The prime goal of any act of learning, aside from the fun we may have in the process, is that it should serve us in the future . . . take us somewhere . . . let us move onward more easily.

Currently, we seem to be miserably caught in the traps of our traditional courses and curricular structures and our foggy dichotomies: Skills versus broad background, humanities versus social science, research versus teaching, theory versus practice, basic versus applied, quantitative versus qualitative, you name it. Again I think we will waste a great deal of time in sterile discussions unless we become explicit. And, we will move nowhere at all unless we are ready to experiment, even if now we experiment only in our imaginations by asking: "What if . . ." One of my points here is that we do not carry out our "liberal backgrounding" responsibility to our students by sending them off to a whole bunch of liberal-arts-outside-of-communication courses, whether these are labeled social science, physical science, humanities or something else. For one thing, there are too damn many courses floating around under such labels which have had no more thought put to them in the last 10 years than some of our own courses. We need rather to ask—What kinds of educational experience, feasible in the university setting, can we discover or help to create which will be most worthwhile for our students?

Much needed is a continuing effort to greatly increase students' knowledge of and sensitivity to similarities and differences among men through time (historically) and through space (culturally). We need to experiment with ways of doing this other than reading books and listening to lectures. I don't suggest that we dispense with the latter, but rather that we try some things like role playing, a year or two of work in a quite different culture, etc. The approach I'm suggesting might better prepare them for mobility and, within a field, for adaption to demands of a changing environment.

This paper has certainly rambled. Many of the ideas are underdeveloped. Even so, they do help me to express my central theme which is: Let us be much less rigidly structured and much more experimental in our approaches; let us come alive; let us explore; let us imagine.

INTRODUCTION

Human Communication Handbook is a collection of experience-based exercises, simulations and instructional games which highlight particular aspects of communication for exploration and study. The book is not primarily about communication theory. Its purpose, on the whole, is to foster and encourage students to engage actively and purposefully in the testing and development of theories of their own communication behavior and human communication behavior in general.

Given such an objective, a fundamental question is: Why be obtuse? Our textbooks and journals are, after all, replete with theories of communication and human behavior. If one's goal is to facilitate theory development and testing, why not simply summarize pertinent theories and enjoin students to test these theories? There are a number of reasons. Some have to do with how people seem best to learn, and some have to do with the nature of human communication.

First, games and simulations involve students directly in the processes they are to learn, and to the extent that there's anything to the adage that "experience is the best teacher," such a method has much to recommend it from the point of view of learning. If one reflects upon points of the significant learning in his or her own life, more often than not, many of those learnings occurred in situations where he was highly involved, and had at least a moderate degree of personal investment. Often, such learning occurs in an extra-curricular context and involves interactions with roommates, friends, members of one's sorority or club, etc. Seldom are such experiences the product of classroom experiences alone. Experience-based learning provides a means for capitalizing upon these more informal learning dynamics. To some extent, at least, it offers a means of bringing them into the classroom, where the dynamics of human communication can be explored in a relevant, yet systematic manner.

There are, additionally, some obvious limits to the extent to which a teacher can inspire students to an understanding of communication phenomena which well match his or her own in terms of depth, breadth, or personal applicability. As with any subject matter, the individual who selects himself to be an instructor or facilitator, by definition, is one who has an unusually high interest in and knowledge of an area. Frequent problems facing the instructor are how to generate enthusiasm for the subject matter and how to illustrate its relevance to the lives of students. Approaches to experiential teaching inject a novelty into the classroom curriculum, and when blended with more traditional instructional methods, the results can be heightened motivation toward a subject-matter area and increased personal relevance of textbook information.

Further, the use of experience-based activities enlarges areas of shared reference between students and instructor. As a consequence, in discussions of particular theories or propositions, examples with which both students and instructor are intimately acquainted can be cited and examined.

Additionally, understanding communication concepts is not the same as being competent to perform consistently with those concepts. Providing students with verbal exposure to theories about communication effectiveness for this or that situation, may be of little or no use in the student's efforts to apply his or her verbal knowledge in their daily lives. Knowing a particular theory of communication—interpersonal, organizational, or mass communication—may in the long run be necessary, but certainly isn't a sufficient condition for being personally effective in such contexts.

Similarly, at a verbal level, many of the basic concepts of communication are incredibly simple. We know, for example, that it is useful to listen carefully to what others are saying in interpersonal communication situations, and in many instances to strive to suppress our own reactions and judgments. Simple to say—not so simple to do. Experiential learning provides a context in which students may strive to identify, explore, and resolve discrepancies between their conceptual understandings and their behavioral skills, hopefully improving both in the process.

A fact not well reflected in many instructional communication systems is that what works communicationally depends largely upon what personal resources one has to work with. Knowing that Walter Cronkite is a more credible source than Richard Nixon has little obvious pertinence to the problems and opportunities facing John Olson (student), who wishes his friends would pay more attention to what he has to say. Improved understanding of how particular communication dynamics operate across large number of individuals, most of the time, may offer little useful information for a given individual who wishes to improve his ability to assess and alter his or her own communicative functioning. Again, experiential instruction affords such an opportunity.

In as much as participants in experience-based learning are involved directly in the analysis of the experiences in which they've participated, there is also a likelihood they will learn to apply these same analytic techniques outside the classroom. With an ongoing commitment to becoming aware of one's own communication behavior and the reactions of others to it, experience becomes a basis for theory-testing and development. In this regard, experience-based teaching is a means of stimulating a learning process which is likely to continue well beyond the classroom and the years of formal education.

Against this backdrop of potential and promise remain a number of persistent—and generally unaddressed—concerns and criticisms. A number of them focus generally on the trainer, instructor, or teacher. All too often, it has been argued, trainers and instructors utilizing games and simulations lack the necessary expertise, familiarity, and background. In many cases, users conceive of experiential methods as the panacea for all problems of education. It has also been pointed out, that largely as a product of the way such activities are used, affective outcomes are more probable than either cognitive or behavioral ones. Partly because of the generally positive responses of students, it is believed users may devote more attention to broadening their repetoire of activities than to considering when, whether, or why to use them.

Other more basic issues of concern focus on the conceptual and historical underpinnings of the field. Considerable attention has been devoted in experiential learning to considering specific activities—games, simulations, structured exercises, the encounter group and other group methods. Considerably less effort has been devoted to developing a framework which explores the similarities between one game and another, between games and simulations, simulations and encounter groups, or simulations and structured exercises. How the design, selection and utilization of experiential techniques can be related to particular instructional objectives, is also an issue of some concern. And, it has been suggested that research is needed to explore the extent to which particular experiential activities are capable of facilitating specific sorts of pedagogical outcomes.

The Structure and Function of Experience-Based Learning Environments

While it is beyond the scope of this book to provide a comprehensive theory of experiential instruction, the following pages present a generic model which aims to: 1) enumerate the forms of experiential activities and their relationship to one another; 2) provide a classification scheme for examining the structural components and interactional dynamics of experiential activities; 3) suggest the relationship between structures of experiential activities and instructional outcomes; 4) indicate the basis by which experiential techniques can be selected and utilized to match instructional objectives.

A Brief History

It is probably important to note, once again, that there's nothing particularly new about the idea of experience-based education, and to briefly indicate a sense of the history of the development of thinking and use of experiential techniques. The conceptual and operational roots of experiential learning date to the work of John Dewey[1] and Maria Montessori,[2] both of whom emphasized the role of experience and communication in classroom learning nearly three quarters of a century ago. The threads of this perspective surface again in the contributions of Jerome Bruner[3] and to a lesser extent in Carl Rogers,[4] both of whom stressed the importance of involving students directly and actively in the processes of learning and inquiry.

The notion of using simulation or gaming for training purposes is not particularly new either. Tansey and Unwin[5] trace their development to war games, and in particular to chess, a symbolic tactical encounter between opposing factions. Early war games were not played for fun alone and served rudimentary instructional and training functions for participants. The popularity of war games increased over time and they were widely used as training devices in World War II, particularly by the Japanese and Germans.[6] Subsequently, the

United States and the Soviet Union also began greater utilization of gaming techniques for war tactical training.[7]

Another important thrust to the development of instructional games and simulations came from business and industry where a growing emphasis was placed upon human relations. The first widely-used management game was developed in 1956 by the American Management Association.

The AMA game consists of five teams of five players each; each team represents the officers of a different firm manufacturing a similar product, competitively sold in a common market.[8]

In addition, the use of games, role playing exercises, and case studies increased greatly within business and industry.[9] Sensitivity training and related experience-based laboratory instructional techniques also grew in popularity.

Also significant in the development of experience-based instructional techniques was work in social psychology on group dynamics and small group interaction. These contributions were to underpin a good deal of the popularity of encounter group and early organizational development techniques, used for instruction in communication, social psychology, business administration, counseling, clinical psychology, social work, and nursing.

In communication, interest in the use of experiential activities has been growing steadily in recent years. In speech, journalism, and mass communication instruction applications are increasingly popular. Especially for instruction in interpersonal, group and intercultural communication, experiential techniques are used to augment and supplement traditional lecture-textbook methods. Simulations and games of one sort or another have also become widely used as the basis of communication research and theory-building, especially in areas of conflict, bargaining, cooperation and competition, and a number of interpersonal, group, and organizational communication contexts.

Experiential techniques come in innumerable packages and with different purposes. All share in common a number of generic structural components which are crucial to their functioning. The five basic conceptual elements are:

1. *Roles*
2. *Interactions*
3. *Rules*
4. *Goals*
5. *Criteria*

Structurally, simulations and games and other experiential designs are composed of: 1) participants cast in *roles;* 2) *interactions* between those roles; 3) *rules* governing the interactions; 4) *goals* with respect to which the interactions occur; and 5) *criteria* for determining the attainment of the goals) and the termination of the activity.

All experience-based instructional systems involve considerations relative to roles, interactions, rules, goals, and criteria, but not all apply these design parameters in the same manner, nor toward the same ends.

Experiential environments can be designed and utilized such that control over the definition and regulation of the five critical parameters is handled in one of two ways. Responsibility for specification of an activity's components may be centralized in the hands of the designer, trainer or instructor, or that control can be dispersed among participants.

Pragmatically, the dimensions of *component structure* and *parameter control* are of considerable importance in the design, selection, and use of all experiential activities because they have implications for how such environments are constructed as well as how, and toward what ends, they operate. At a conceptual level, these same factors are also crucial since they provide a basis for developing a generalized model and classification of experiential instruction.

In the discussion that follows, each of these dimensions, and their relationship to one another, will be considered in depth. The *component structure* dimension will be discussed in terms of *roles, rules, interactions, goals,* and *criteria,* as noted previously. Each will be defined, and their nature and function in a variety of games, simulations, and exercises, will be explored. The *parameter control* dimension will be considered in terms of two modes of control: *external* and *internal* parameters, and the implications of the distinction will be discussed.

Roles

Obviously experiential environments require participants, and except for those unique situations in which one participant "plays" against himself, there are always two or more individuals involved. Participants assume roles—the identities taken on while taking part in a simulation, game, etc. The origins and importance of role definitions depends upon the design of the activity.

In a number of games and role playing exercises, rather definitive and elaborate role descriptions are provided by the designer. In SENSITIVITY,[10] for example, a portfolio containing a fictionalized biographical sketch is distributed to each player. Participants are asked to assume the role of the character described in the folio as best they can. The structural element of role is particularly crucial to this game, and all player activities revolve around their actions and reactions to one another in their assumed roles.

The players, taken all together then, become a group of very troubled people, who meet to gain some help and insights from each other. Each tries to make his character understandable to the group, communicating as much about himself and his problems as he can.[11]

SIMSOC[12] is an example of a more complex social simulation in which prescriptive roles, specified in great detail, are extremely important from both an operational and instructional standpoint. SIMSOC participants serve in roles in one of seven basic groups. Two of the groups are industrial units, and two are political parties. The other three are: an employee interest group, a mass media group and a judicial council. Additionally, a specified proportion of participants in the simulated society must be affiliated with one of the two political units and with the group of independents. Members of the Party of the People (POP) are told that they are to emphasize individual autonomy and decentralized decision-making. "They are not rigid about such opposition, and are willing to accept planning and centralized coordination if it appears *absolutely necessary.*"[13]

Members of the Society Party (POP) are encouraged to emphasize central planning. "Its members believe that it is necessary for individuals and groups to yield some of their autonomy in order that effective leadership be provided and anarchy avoided."[14] Independents are told they have no strong opinions one way or another about these issues.

Both SENSITIVITY and SIMSOC are examples of experience-based systems in which role definitions are prescribed rather specifically and have a crucial, and generally predictable, impact on the overall operation of the activity.

SOCIETY[15] or the encounter group, in idealized form, represent experience-based environments, which differs dramatically with respect to the origin of the role definitions participants assume. In these cases, roles—the way participants are to act—are not specified on an *a priori* basis, nor are they prescribed by the designer, but rather are defined by the participants themselves. Similar activities, though a bit less extreme in terms of role definition are PRISONERS DILEMMA[16] and some versions of WIN AS MUCH AS YOU CAN.[17] In each context, the nature of participant roles emerge primarily as a product of what players bring with them to the activity, and as a consequence of the interpersonal transactions that occur as the activity progresses.

STAR POWER[18] provides an example of a structured environment which falls somewhere between the two extremes, with regard to role delineation, tending somewhat toward the less specified, less structured end of the continuum.

Interactions

The operation of all games and simulations depends upon the interrelating of participants and roles. The manner in which these relationships originate and develop varies from one game or simulation to the next as do the methods, procedures, and channels available for transactions between players.

The "classic" MONOPOLY, for example, utilizes a large number of devices to foster interactions between players including tokens, play money, houses, hotels, property deed cards, community chest, and chance cards. The availability and necessity of using multiple channels of communication, so crucial to the functioning of MONOPOLY, are central in many instructional games and simulations as well.

In some games and simulations interaction channels and means for their utilization are less elaborate, prescribed, and specified than in MONOPOLY. This is, for example, the case with most role playing exercises, where a wide range of verbal and nonverbal interactions are available to players as a part of the activity. The range and diversity of transactions between player roles are limited more by the limits of a participant's ingenuity than by the design of the game or exercise.

HANG-UP[19] is a role-playing game which utilizes reasonably diverse channels of interaction to focus upon and increase participant sensitivity to subtleties of racial difference. In the game, participants react to a series of hypothetical "crisis situations," described on cards, as they think typical whites or blacks would. In turn, participants simulate their reactions to the various crisis situations while others involved in the game try to guess the player's "hang-up," and whether he is playing the role of a white or black. With HANG-UP participants are constrained to utilize only non-verbal channels for interaction; and the manner and timing of the exchanges are regulated quite precisely by the game design.

INTERACT, INTERACT II,[20] and INTERMEDIA[21] provide instances of simulations which utilizes emergent interaction channels. Both simulations involve a laboratory society, the basic industries of which are communication and mass communication enterprises. Participants function as members of Mass Communication Organizations, Communication Agencies or an Executive Council. In addition, all participants serve as consumers for communication products developed by the various communication organizations.

The communication organizations negotiate, prepare, and distribute communication products to the consumers, according to a predetermined timetable. The consumers are exposed to and in turn evaluate the products of each communication organization relative to one another, and award income or subsistence points based upon their assessments. The points each communication organization accumulates are distributed among the members of its group in whatever manner the organization determines to be appropriate.

In addition to this basic pattern of interaction, any individual or group of individuals can provide any communication product or service to any group within the society so long as they are able to accumulate enough income points for their efforts to survive in the economy of the simulated society. In experiential activities such as this, multiple interactions occur, utilizing verbal, non-verbal, print and broadcast channels. Only the minimal set of interactions are specified by the game design; others are a consequence of participant-initiated patterns.

Rules

The interactions between participant roles in experiential contexts are governed by a series of rules or guidelines. Rules are typically specified by the designer and presented to the player as "instructions" for play. The number and specificity of rules governing the interactions vary greatly from one experiential activity to the next. Rules may enumerate actions which are permitted of players, or they may list only those activities which are precluded, leaving open the possibility of all other actions.

This distinction is an important one. Those rules which specify and enumerate actions and behaviors which are permitted and necessary for participants can be termed prescriptive rules. Those which prohibit certain actions leaving all other possible behaviors open are proscriptive rules.

In some instances, the designer utilizes the rules and behavioral patterns players bring to the situation as a primary source of rules for the game or simulation exercise. SOCIETY, or the encounter group, may be the best examples of this variety of rule generation, particularly where one conceives of these activities as simulations of the processes involved in social organizing. Rules are generated from the participants' assumptions as to how a group or society should organize and toward what ends this organization ought to occur. Similarly, participants determine through play what behaviors ought to be tolerated, encouraged, institutionalized, etc. At a minimum, several meta-rules must be imposed by the instructor. Minimally, individuals must, for example, agree to participate—at least initially—in the formation of the group, organization, or society.

In other sorts of experience-based instructional exercises, traditional and direct means for interactions between participants are intentionally excluded by the rules in order to highlight particular aspects of the communication process or to focus upon particular issues. This is the case with the COOPERATION SQUARES EXERCISE[22] which has the following rules:

1. No member may speak.
2. No member may ask for a card or in any way signal that he wants one.
3. Members may give cards to others.

Participants in this exercise are divided into five-person groups. Each group member receives an envelope containing several puzzle pieces. When assembled, the pieces possessed by the members of the group form five equal squares. No one member of a team has all the cards necessary to complete a puzzle-square. Only through exchanging pieces with other participants can the task be completed.

The exercise and the discussion which follows is intended to focus upon the issues involved in communication and effective cooperation, and to help participants become more aware of how particular behaviors may facilitate or retard group problem-solving.

Goals

While goals are crucial to the design and implementation of experience-based activities in general, the extent to which they are overtly presented to participants varies greatly from one simulation or game to the next.

In the COOPERATION SQUARES EXERCISE discussed previously, the activity goal is stated rather directly:

> Each person should have an envelope containing pieces for forming squares. At the signal, the task of the group is to form five squares of equal size. The task is not complete until everyone has before him a perfect square and all the squares are the same size.[23]

Often the goal of an exercise, game, or simulation is given in the instructions, stated as "the objectives" of the game. Where two or more individuals are involved, the goal may take the form of a statement of what one must do "to win."

In contradistinction, the goals of an encounter group, SOCIETY—or to a lesser extent of simulations such as INTERACT, COMMUNICATION SYS-

16 Human Communication Handbook

TEMS SIMULATION or HYPOTHETICA[24]—depend primarily upon the decisions participants make, and often emerge at a point well into the development of the activity. In such situations, the goals may never be articulated in the group as a whole, and it is not necessary for each individual's goal(s) to be identical with the goals of other participants.

Somewhere between these two extremes are games and simulations with multiple goals, prescribed by the designer. BAFA-BAFA,[25] CULTURE I, and CULTURE II,[26] Intercultural Communication simulations, and SIMSOC, are examples. In BAFA-BAFA participants function in one of two simulated cultures—one which is highly task-oriented, another which is more person-oriented. In the process of playing out one of the two cultural roles—and visiting and interacting with members of the other culture—a variety of goals are served. CULTURE I involves participants in the creation of a hypothetical culture. CULTURE II interfaces members of the culture with representatives from another culture to consider the relative personal and social merits of merger versus continued isolationism.

In SIMSOC all participants pursue multiple goals in one of two political parties—or as an independent. The *Participant's Manual*[27] indicates:

If you are assigned to one of the two political parties, you are to consider the achievement of the party's program one of your own personal goals and to work for this when it appears appropriate to do so.

In addition to participation in one of the seven basic groups with attendant goals, and political affiliation with additional specified goals, each participant must also select one of three personal goals—power, wealth or popularity—to emphasize in playing the game. A participant seeking power tries to influence what happens in the society, those electing to seek wealth try to accumulate much of the currency of the society, while others emphasize popularity and strive to become well liked by other simulation participants.

Criteria

Experiential activities must have a means of ending. A determination is made that the goals have been reached using certain criteria and this signals the end of activity. Some games and simulations rely heavily upon the use of fixed and prescribed criteria for determining when goals have been met and activity is to terminate. Others make use of the ambiguity that results when criteria for determining the achievement of goals are unclear, changing, and highly personal. The criteria can be prescribed by the designer in advance, or may emerge from the decisions of players.

In games where the goal is rather directly stated, often in terms of winning, the criterion is typically an announcement by a participating individual that in his or her assessment the goal has been fulfilled. "Bingo!" is perhaps the clearest example. A pronouncement of this sort is also used with the COOPERATION SQUARES EXERCISE.

In other cases the criterion for determining when the goal has been reached depends upon time constraints. This is the case in an encounter group, or

INTERACT, where the length of time available is a primary factor in determining the termination of activity. Some activities such as BAFA-BAFA, CULTURE I, and CULTURE II end when all participants have been cycled through particular roles. Others, such as STARPOWER are terminated at the discretion of the facilitator with or without input from participants.

Parameter Control

In the foregoing discussion, it was suggested that experience-based environments may differ from one another in terms of the origins, locus of control, and function of their structural components. Where primary control over the definition and regulation of parameters relative to roles, rules, interactions, goals, and criteria, originates and resides with the designer or facilitator, the environment can be said to be *externally parametered*. Where this authority and responsibility is diffused among participants, the activity is *internally parametered*. Externally-parametered games and simulations are those simulations, games, and structured exercises where the participant essentially strives to replicate the designer's theory of a particular phenomenon or process. The participant in externally-parametered environments typically explores various behavioral or conceptual strategies and procedures in an effort to arrive at the predetermined correct or winning action or behaviors, set by the designer or instructor.

Externally-parametered activities tend to include relatively simple, low ambiguity situations, with specified and prescribed roles. The "right" and "wrong" strategies for behaving and interacting are fixed, or systematically varied in known ways, under the control of the designer or user and the criteria for winning are externally imposed.

Given this configuration, since the problems with which a participant deals, and the appropriate solutions to them have been determined on an *a priori* basis by the designer, they are little affected by the actions or reactions of the participants. The correct strategies for play are essentially the same from one iteration of the game or simulation to the next. When emphasizing discovery of the correct ordering of items needed for existence on the moon, the NASA EXERCISE,[28] provides a reasonably good example of an externally-parametered activity.

While games and simulations which are more or less externally parametered are numerous, there are fewer activities with internal parameters. In the internally parametered design, what it is that is to be learned, and the ways the learning is to occur are often not specified or wholly predetermined by a designer or instructor, but rather may depend almost entirely upon what the participants decide to do and the ways in which they arrive at those decisions. Variation in problem-naming and problem-solving is tolerated—even encouraged—in such an experiential system. Correct strategies and goals for the activity are defined largely through interactants thoughts and actions, rather than being imposed by the design of the activity.

TABLE 1
Structural Elements and Design Characteristics of Experiential Learning Systems

	Parameters	
	External	**Internal**
Roles	assigned rigid low ambiguity simple	emergent flexible high ambiguity complex
Interactions	channels specified patterns prescribed low ambiguity few channels available predictable	channels emerge patterns emerge high ambiguity multiple channels available unpredictable
Rules	prescriptive fixed constant low ambiguity specified	proscriptive flexible changing high ambiguity emergent
Goals	imposed uniform single clearly defined	emergent individual multiple ambiguously defined
Criteria	predictable uniform singular likely to involve "winning" clearly defined	unpredictable individual multiple unlikely to involve "winning" ambiguously defined

Implications for Design and Utilization

The manner in which experience-based instructional environments can be dissected and analyzed in terms of their structural components and the nature and origin of parameter control, has been indicated in the foregoing discussion. It may now be illustrative to consider how this sort of analysis can be useful in designing, selecting, and utilizing experiential activities to coincide with particular instructional objectives.

There are, of course, a variety of ways to go about designing, or deciding whether to use, a particular game, simulation, structured exercise, or variant group activity. In varying sequence and with differential weightings for significance, one considers the number of participants, the nature of the participant group, availability of resources, time constraints, what activities will precede and follow the one in question, predictability of outcomes of particular exercises, etc. The facilitator/trainer strives to design and select activities which satisfactorily accommodate each of these variables in a manner that he or she believes to be appropriate.

Over-arching this sort of planning and decision-making are more basic and fundamental considerations relative to training or instructional goals: When to use experiential methods and when straight-forward informational sessions; when to use one sort of game, simulation, or exercise, and when another; when to provide a structured facilitator-centered debriefing and when to let participants determine directions of discussion.

It is with regard to generic considerations of goals and objectives—and the myriad of related issues, questions, and procedures—that the suggested classification scheme has most relevance. How components of experiential activities are structured and regulated has rather direct consequence for the sorts of goals that might profitably be pursued with their use.

It is the nature of components and the sources of their control which seem most clearly, to distinguish the more content-oriented learning systems from those matched to goals of individualized, process-oriented instruction. In general, experiential activities with components that are externally defined and regulated—externally parametered—seem appropriate to instructional settings where the teaching of specific content is the primary goal. Conversely, activities that are more internally parametered seem better suited for instruction in more generalized coping processes.

Where the learning goals suggest that what is to be taught tends to be *specific, prescribable, predictable, specifiable,* and *determinant,* externally-parametered systems are logical. Here the designer or user desires all students to learn the same target facts, strategies, and procedures—content—in the same way. The structural elements of the activity—roles, interactions, rules, goals, criteria—will need therefore, to be controlled and manipulated purposefully, to insure as much as possible, that all interactants deal with the intended content.

Take, for example, a role playing exercise designed to help students learn the content of a particular theory, experientially. The structural elements of the activity would need to be managed such that participants were unlikely to introduce "creativity" into the exercise. Any departure in learning might lead them to arrive at a "theory" quite different from the one about which they were supposed to be learning. If, for example, a role-playing situation were developed to demonstrate how, in an interpersonal context, self-disclosure by one individual tends to foster self-disclosure by another, it would be essential to design the role and interaction components to insure that one party engaged in self-disclosing behavior at the outset. Similarly, if the goal of a game or simulation were to provide participants with a sense of the differences between communication outcomes where feedback is present, and where it is not, it is critical for the user or designer to provide rules and goal specifications which more or less guarantee the result.

Thus, externally-parametered designs are generally appropriate when the instructional objectives are to teach particular theories, whether of interpersonal, group, organizational or cross-cultural communication.

Internally-parametered designs, on the other hand, are better suited to situations where the instructional goals are *structural, process-oriented, generic, variable, indeterminant,* and *not fully prescribable.*

TABLE 2
Training/Instructional Goals and Parameter Control

Parameters

External Parameters	Internal Parameters
content-oriented	process-oriented
particular theories	theory-building
specific	generic
prescribable	not prescribable
predictable	indeterminant
specifiable	variable
determined	

Meta Goals

homogeneity	heterogeneity
uniformity	diversity
interchangeability	individual uniqueness

If a goal is to teach students the theory-building—as opposed to a particular theory—internally-parametered designs are more appropriate. Experiential activities intended to teach processes—rather than theory content—of intrapersonal, interpersonal, group, or organizational communication dynamics and decision-making, might utilize a concensus activity like the NASA exercise, but to a different end. In this case, since that which is to be learned is a process, arriving at a particular ranking or the learning of specific content or outcomes would be irrelevant and perhaps dysfunctional. Given this kind of learning goal, creativity is highly desirable—and all participants need not learn the same things about survival on the moon, communication, concensus or decision-making. Neither, in such a case, is it necessary or desirable for all of the individuals to depart from the experience with identical conclusions as to what was "right" and what was "wrong."

It is suggested then, that in general, the more internally-parametered designs are best suited for teaching, questioning, inquiry, and for helping individuals develop *their own* theories of dynamics, leadership, group decision-making, interpersonal, social, organizational, and cross-cultural communication. The validity of such skills and knowledges are situational, and depend upon one's own unique abilities and competencies as well as the needs and capacities of other persons who have a stake in the outcomes of particular interactions. A judgment of "rightness" or "wrongness" of a particular problem-naming or problem-solving style, or a manner of coping with other people, is most appropriately made relative to the purposes of the individuals involved and their situation. The emergence of criteria for such judgments is possible when a design tends toward internal parameters. Where parameters are external, such criteria remain fixed from one set of participants and behaviors to the next.

There are several additional dimensions which are useful for distinguishing between circumstances appropriate to the use of externally and internally parametered simulations and games. These relate to learning system meta-goals and philosophies. Where the attempt within an instructional system is toward fostering *homogeneity, uniformity,* and *interchangeability* among students, external parameters are in order. Again, by way of distinction, internal parameters seem to better fit where the environment seeks to encourage *heterogeneity, diversity,* and *individual uniqueness*.

While much of the foregoing discussion has focused directly upon the design and selection of experiential activities, implications of the framework for considering their implementation, are closely related. Where one's training goals suggest the selection of the more externally parametered sorts of activities, debriefing format and style should be designed to maximize the transfer of specified information to participants. The more predictably participants come to a shared understanding of their learnings, and the more closely those understandings match those of the instructor/facilitator, the more effective the outcome. Discussion should strive to augment these ends.

Where the over-arching goals of the facilitator correspond more closely with those suggested for internally parametered activities, somewhat different procedures and strategies may be employed in discussion during or following the activity. Here the concern is to encourage participants to deal with the definitions of roles, rules, interactions, goals, and criteria as they emerge in the dynamics of participation. The problem that participants define and view as important, and the ways they find appropriate to solve them, may vary from one individual to the next. The facilitative role in discussion may often be more consultant than teacher. Thus the over-riding goal of debriefing in such instances is to heighten participants introspective capacities and their ability to analyze their own behavior, its differential effects on others, and unconsidered alternatives that were available. The facilitative role in discussion may, therefore, often be more consultant than teacher.

In many respects, the manner in which an experiential activity is implemented and debriefing conducted is more critical to its outcome than are properties inherent in the activity. As with the NASA Exercise mentioned previously, one activity can be used effectively to two quite different ends, largely as a consequence of how debriefing is conducted. Thus, implementation strategy may conceivably reinforce, neutralize, or reverse the mode of parameter control and outcomes of instruction. That this is the case, serves to underscore the importance of attending very carefully to the influences of parameter control in the use as well as selection and design of experiential activities.

No theory of experience-based instruction can be prescriptive. When considering issues of design, selection, and implementation of experiential activities it is useful to remind oneself, at least in passing, that all learning environments are, to some extent, participant controlled whether that control is delegated explicitly or not. What an individual learns and the way that learning occurs always depends ultimately upon the capacities, values, interests, goals, and understandings of the learner. The game designer or user provides the necessary, but not sufficient conditions for learning.

The Communication Framework

It is an objective of this *Human Communication Handbook* to facilitate those who wish to explore the uses of experiential learning in communication instruction, and to augment the resources of those who have, for some time, been applying such methods in their teaching. Included in the volume are exercises, games, and simulations each of which has been carefully selected, designed, and/or redesigned to focus upon reasonably central communication concepts and personal applications of them.

While experience-based learning has been discussed it might be useful to discuss briefly the framework underlying the organization of this book. The contents fall into four sections: 1) Intrapersonal Communication, 2) Interpersonal and Social Communication, 3) Cross-cultural, and 4) Mass Communication.

One way to think about human communication is that it focuses first upon the individual and the nature of intrapersonal communication. It is through intrapersonal communication that each individual transacts with his or her environment and, in so doing, attaches meaning and significance to the persons, things, and events around them. This view implies a concern not only for how one communicates-to others, but also how one is communicated-with. Similarly, it suggests that communication involves not only what an individual does, says or intends, but also with the whole range of intended and unintended consequences and significances which may be attached to his behavior by others. Conceived in this manner, it is clear that one's failure to speak may indeed have as much communicative consequence as the opposite. If I leave out something from this section of discussion which a reader thought should have been included, the omission may be interpreted in any one of a variety of ways, none of which may bear any relationship to what I said or intended. From this view of communication, the focus is upon the initiation, reception, and interpretation of messages—whether spoken, non-verbal, or written.

When the level of analysis shifts from the individual and intrapersonal communication, to the nature, intents, and consequences of the communicative relationship between two or more persons, the focus may be termed interpersonal or social communication. Whether in a classroom, a gathering of friends, a marriage, or a society, communication provides and maintains the links between people which make social organization and cooperation possible. It is, of course, through social communication (in one form or another) that we acquire and share our knowledge, attitudes, beliefs, values, and opinions of the present and past. Processes involved in the initiation, transmission, and interpretation of messages in dyads, groups, organizations, and societies are included in Section II of the volume.

Cross-cultural is a sub-category of social communication. It involves the sending and receiving of messages by persons from diverse cultural backgrounds. In such situations the languages, customs, rituals, religions, political and economic orientations, and styles of interaction may be grossly different for the persons involved, which intensifies both the challenges and problems of coordinating meanings among them.

Mass Communication evolves out of the interface of intrapersonal and social communication. It involves the production of messages by one or a few persons for distribution and interpretation to a larger audience. Activities included in this section of the handbook explore this process. At a pragmatic level mass communication embodies most of the dynamics explored in other sections of the volume, however, activities in this section provide more focused perspective on information acquisition, interviewing, writing, editing, and gatekeeping, considered in the context of individuals striving to impact or inform members of a large and diverse audience.

Using the Human Communication Handbook

Depending upon one's goals, the participants, and the demands of the situation, the exercises in this book may be used as the basis for a total program in human communication or as supplementary activities in other instructional or training programs. The exercises are suitable for use in sequential order or any other ordering which fits the instructional objectives of a particular situation.

The handbook is designed so that generally, as one moves through it, the exercises progress in complexity and sophistication. Activities in the early portion of the volume are generally designed to make rather specific points or direct attention to fundamental issues about human communication. As one moves to later activities the exercises are intended to allow participants to have an increasing impact upon the directions and outcomes of activity, and the role of the instructor or facilitator shifts from primarily information-giver to discussion leader and question raiser. These later activities require a greater commitment by both participants and instructor.

In addition to the four sections of simulations and games, there is also a section providing observation guides, which are intended for use by participants and/or instructor to help identify and record communication dynamics which occur while using the activities presented in the book.

An additional section of the volume provides a selective bibliography of relevant readings in human communication, experience-based learning, games, simulations, and structured exercises.

References

1. Readers interested in pursuing these notions in depth may wish to examine *John Dewey: Lectures in the Philosophy of Education, 1899* by Reginald D. Archambault (New York: Random House, 1966), especially Lectures VI and VII, pp. 59-75.

   On pages 65-66 of that volume Dewey says: "There seems a very practical existing tendency in the direction of the recognition of this principle, that fundamentally speaking, the educative process must be the same within and without the school walls. . . . When we say the materials and methods are the same it is not that all distinction must be wiped out or overlooked, but it does mean that the school has for its function the organization in a more conscious and thorough going way the resources and the methods and materials that are used in the more unconscious and haphazard way outside."

   See also John Dewey, *Experience and Education* (New York: Macmillan, 1938) and *Democracy and Education* (New York: The Free Press, 1916).
2. Readers interested in writings of Maria Montessori may wish to examine *The Montessori Method* (New York: Shocken Books, 1964) and *Spontaneous Activity in Education* (New York: Shocken Books, 1965).
3. See especially *The Relevance of Education*, J. S. Bruner (New York: W. W. Norton & Co., 1971); *Learning About Learning: A Conference Report*, J. S. Bruner (ed.) (Washington: U.S. Government Printing Office, 1966); J. S. Bruner, *The Process of Education* (Cambridge, Mass.: Harvard Press, 1961); J. S. Bruner, *Toward a Theory of Instruction* (New York: Norton, 1966); and J. S. Bruner, Rose R. Oliver and Patricia M. Greenfield, et al., *Studies in Cognitive Growth* (New York: John Wiley & Sons, 1966).
4. See especially *Encounter Groups*, Carl Rogers (New York: Harper and Row, 1970); "The Characteristics of a Helping Relationship," excerpted from *On Becoming a Person* by Carl Rogers (Boston: Houghton Mifflin, 1961), Chapter 3, pp. 39-58; Carl Rogers, *Freedom to Learn* (Columbus, Ohio: Charles E. Merrill Publishing Co., 1969); Carl Rogers, "Interpersonal Relationships: U.S.A. 2000." This paper was part of a symposium sponsored by the Esalen Institute, San Francisco, entitled "USA 2000" on January 10, 1968. See also Carl R. Rogers, "The Process of the Basic Encounter Group."
5. P. J. Tansey and Derick Unwin, *Simulations and Gaming in Education* (London: Metheun Education, Ltd., 1969), p. 1.
6. John R. Raser, *Simulation and Society: An Exploration of Scientific Gaming* (Boston: Allyn and Bacon, 1969), p. 1.
7. *Ibid.*, p. 47.
8. *Ibid.*, p. 54.

9. Role playing was first used by J. L. Moreno as a psychotherapeutic technique which he termed psychodrama. Patients acted out their personal and interpersonal conflicts within a group of fellow patients. Roles were switched periodically in an attempt to foster among patients a better understanding of their own difficulties and those of others. Role playing, group therapy, sensitivity training and numerous experience-based structured exercises reflect the influences of Moreno's developmental work. For additional background materials see *Psychodrama,* Moreno, J. L., Vol. I, Beacon House, New York, 1946, and *Group Psychotherapy: A Symposium,* J. L. Moreno (ed.), Beacon House, New York, 1945.

    For more discussion of specific applications of role playing, structured exercises, games and simulations in business and industry see William R. Dill, James R. Jackson and James W. Sweeney, *Proceedings on the Conference on Business Games* (New Orleans: Tulane University, 1961), especially Chapter 1.
10. The game *Sensitivity* was designed and developed by Jonah Kalb and David Viscott in 1969 and is distributed by Sensitivity Games, Inc. of Boston.
11. "Instructions," the game of *Sensitivity.*
12. William A. Gamson, *SIMSOC: Participant's Manual* (New York: The Free Press, 1969) and *SIMSOC: Instructor's Manual* (New York: The Free Press).
13. Gamson, *op. cit.,* p. 13.
14. *Ibid.,* p. 13.
15. Described in detail in Brent D. Ruben and Richard W. Budd, *Human Communication Handbook: Simulations and Games.* (Rochelle Park, N.J.: Hayden Book Co., Inc., 1975).
16. *Ibid.*
17. Described in detail in J. William Pfeiffer and John E. Jones, *A Handbook of Structured Experiences for Human Relations Training,* Vol. 2 (La Jolla, Calif.: University Associates, 1969).
18. *Starpower* was developed by R. Garry Shirts and is distributed by Western Behavioral Science Institute.
19. The game of *Hang-Up* is distributed by the Unitarian Universalist Association of Boston.
20. Described in detail in Brent D. Ruben, *Interact II,* (Wayne, N.J.: Avery Publishing Group, 1977).
21. Brent D. Ruben, Albert D. Talbott, Lee M. Brown, and Henry G. LaBrie, *Intermedia* (La Jolla, Calif.: University Associates, 1970). Presented in scaled-down format in Brent D. Ruben and Richard W. Budd, *op. cit.*
22. Described in detail in D. J. Mial and S. Jacobson, *Ten Interaction Exercises for the Classroom,* Washington: National Training Labs, and Brent D. Ruben and Richard W. Budd, *op. cit.*
23. D. J. Mial and S. Jacobson, *op. cit.*

24. Brent D. Ruben and Richard W. Budd, *op. cit.*
25. *Bafa Bafa* was developed by R. Garry Shirts and is distributed by the Western Behavioral Science Institute.
26. Described in detail in this volume.
27. William A. Gamson, *op. cit.*, p. 13.
28. J. William Pfeiffer and John E. Jones, *A Handbook of Structured Experiences for Human Relations Training,* Vol. 1, (La Jolla, Calif.: University Associates, 1969).

Bibliography

Collateral Readings in Intrapersonal, Social, Intercultural and Mass Communication

Allport, Gordon W., *Personality and Social Encounter*, Boston: Beacon Press, 1960.
Aranguren, José L., *Human Communication*, New York: McGraw-Hill, 1967.
Argyle, Michael, *Social Interaction*, New York: Atherton, 1969.
Baker, Larry L. and Robert J. Kibler, *Speech Communication Behavior*, Englewood Cliffs, N.J.: Prentice-Hall, 1971.
Barnhart, Sara A., *Introduction to Interpersonal Communication*, New York: Crowell, 1976.
Barnlund, Dean C., *Interpersonal Communication*, Boston: Houghton Mifflin, 1968.
Bennis, Warren C., *Changing Organizations*, New York: McGraw-Hill, 1966.
Bennis, Warren, E. H. Schein, F. I. Steel, and D. E. Berlew, *Interpersonal Dynamics*, Homewood, Ill.: Dorsey-Irwin, 1968.
Berger, Peter L., and Thomas Luckmann, *The Social Construction of Reality*, New York: Doubleday, 1966.
Berlo, David Kenneth, *The Process of Communication*, New York: Holt, Rinehart, and Winston, 1960.
Bion, W. R., *Experience in Groups*, New York: Basic Books, 1969.
Birdwhistell, Ray L., *Kinesics and Context*, Philadelphia: University of Pennsylvania Press, 1970.
Blumer, Herbert, *Symbolic Interactionism*, Englewood Cliffs, N.J.: Prentice-Hall, 1969.
Bois, J. S., *The Art of Awareness*, Dubuque, Iowa: W. C. Brown, 1970.
Bormann, E. G. and N. C. Bormann, *Effective Small Group Communication*, Minneapolis, Minn.: Burgess Publishing Co., 1972.
Boulding, Kenneth, *The Image*, Ann Arbor: University of Michigan Press, 1960.
Britt, Stewart H., *Consumer Behavior and the Behavioral Sciences*, New York: Wiley, 1966.
Brooks, William D., *Speech Communication*, Dubuque, Iowa: W. C. Brown, 1971.
Brooks, William D. and Philip Emert, *Interpersonal Communication*, Dubuque, Iowa: Wm. C. Brown, 1976.
Brown, Roger W., *Words and Things*, New York: Free Press, 1958.
Budd, Richard W. and Brent D. Ruben, *Approaches to Human Communication*, Rochelle Park, N.J.: Hayden, 1972.
Burgoon, Michael, Judy Heston, and James McCroskey, *Small Group Communication*, New York: Holt, Rinehart, Winston, 1974.
Burke, Kenneth, *Language as Symbolic Action*, Berkeley, Calif.: University of California Press, 1966.

Burke, Kenneth, *Permanence and Change,* New York: The New Republic, 1935.
Burton, Arthur, *Encounter,* San Francisco, Calif.: Jossey-Bass, 1970.
Campbell, James and Hal W. Hepler, *Dimensions in Communication: Readings,* Belmont, Calif.: Wadsworth Pub. Co., 1970.
Capp, Glen R., *Basic Oral Communication,* Englewood Cliffs, N.J.: Prentice-Hall, 1971.
Carpenter, Edmund S. and Marshall McLuhan, *Explorations in Communication,* Boston: Beacon Press, 1966.
Carroll, John B., *Language and Thought,* Englewood Cliffs, N.J.: Prentice-Hall, 1964.
Cathcart, Robert S. and Larry A. Samovar, *Small Group Communication,* Dubuque, Iowa: W. C. Brown, 1970.
Chronkite, Gary, *Communication and Awareness,* Menlo Park, Calif.: Cummings Press, 1976.
Church, J., *Language and the Discovery of Reality,* New York: Random House, 1961.
Civickly, Jean M., *Messages,* New York: Random House, 1974.
Cohen, Joseph, *Group Dynamics,* New York: Rand McNally, 1971.
Condon, John C. and Fathi Yousef, *An Introduction to Intercultural Communication,* Indianapolis: Bobbs-Merrill, 1975.
Dance, Frank E. X. and Carl E. Larson, *The Functions of Human Communication,* New York: Holt, Rinehart, Winston, 1976.
Dance, Frank E. X., *Human Communication Theory,* New York: Holt, Rinehart and Winston, 1967.
Dance, Frank E. and Carl E. Larson, *Speech Communication,* New York: Holt, Rinehart and Winston, 1972.
DeFleur, Melvin L. and Sandra Ball-Rokeach, *Theories of Mass Communication,* New York: McKay, 1975.
DeFleur, Melvin L., and Otto N. Larsen, *The Flow of Information,* New York: Harper, 1958.
DeFleur, Melvin L., *Theories of Mass Communication,* New York: David McKay, 1970.
Deutsch, Karl W., *Nationalism and Social Communication,* Cambridge, Mass.: M.I.T. Press, 1966.
DeVito, J. A., *Communication Concepts and Processes,* Englewood, Cliffs, N.J.: Prentice-Hall, 1971.
DeVito, Joseph, *Communication,* Englewood Cliffs, N.J.: Prentice-Hall, 1971.
Dexter, Lewis A., and David Manning White, *People, Society and Mass Communications,* New York: Free Press, 1964.
Diedrich, R. C. and H. A. Dye, *Group Procedures: Purposes, Processes and Outcomes,* Boston, Houghton Mifflin, 1972.
Dorsey, J. M. and W. H. Seegers, *Living Consciously,* Detroit: Wayne State Press, 1959.
Duncan, Hugh Dalziel, *Communication and Social Order,* New York: Oxford University Press, 1969.

Duncan, Hugh Dalziel, *Symbols and Social Theory,* New York: Oxford University Press, 1962.
Duncan, Hugh Dalziel, *Symbols in Society,* New York: Oxford University Press, 1968.
Efron, David, *Gesture and Environment,* New York: King's Crown Press, 1941.
Eisenberg, Abne M. and Ralph R. Smith, Jr., *Nonverbal Communication,* Indianapolis, Indiana: Bobbs-Merrill, 1971.
Emery, Edwin, Phillip H. Ault, and Warren Agee, *Introduction to Mass Communications,* New York: Dodd, Mead, 1970.
Emery, Michael C. and Ted C. Smythe, *Readings in Mass Communications,* Dubuque, Iowa: W. C. Brown, 1972.
Fabun, Don, *Communications,* New York: Glencoe Press, 1971.
Fagen, Richard R., *Politics and Communication,* Boston: Little, Brown, 1966.
Farrar, Ronald T., and John D. Stevens, *Mass Media and the National Experience,* New York: Harper and Row, 1971.
Foote, Nelson S., and L. S. Cottrell, Jr., *Identity and Interpersonal Competence,* Chicago: University of Chicago Press, 1965.
Foundation for Research on Human Behavior, *Communication in Organizations,* Ann Arbor, Mich.: University of Michigan Press, 1959.
Frings, H., and M. Frings, *Animal Communication,* New York: Blaisdell, 1964.
Gerald, James E., *The Social Responsibility of the Press,* Minneapolis: University of Minnesota Press, 1963.
Gerth, Hans, and C. Wright Mills, *Character and Social Structure,* New York: Harcourt, Brace, 1953.
Giffin, Kim and Bobby R. Patton, *Fundamentals of Interpersonal Communication,* New York: Harper & Row, 1971.
Goffman, Erving, *Behavior in Public Places,* New York: Free Press, 1963.
Goffman, Erving, *Interaction Ritual,* Garden City, New York: Doubleday, Anchor Books, 1967.
Goffman, Erving, *Strategic Interaction,* Philadelphia: University of Pennsylvania Press, 1969.
Goffman, Erving, *The Presentation of Self in Everyday Life,* Garden City, N.Y.: Doubleday, 1959.
Goldhaber, Gerald, *Organizational Communication,* Dubuque, Iowa: W. C. Brown, 1974.
Gordon, George N., *The Language of Communication,* New York: Hastings House, 1969.
Grant, Barbara M., *Moves: An Analysis of Non-verbal Activity,* New York: Teachers College Press, Columbia University, 1971.
Grove, Theodore G., *Experiences in Interpersonal Communication,* Englewood, Cliffs, N.J.: Prentice-Hall, 1976.
Gulley, Halbert E., *Discussion, Conference and Group Process,* New York: Holt, Rinehart & Winston, 1960.
Hall, Edward T., *The Hidden Dimension,* Garden City, N.Y.: Doubleday, 1966.
Hall, Edward T., *The Silent Language,* Garden City, New York: Doubleday, 1959.

Haney, William V., *Communication and Organizational Behavior*, Homewood, Ill.: Richard D. Irwin, 1967.
Hanneman, Gerhard J. and William J. McEwen, eds., *Communication and Behavior*, Reading, Mass.: Addison-Wesley, 1974.
Hayakawa, S. I., *Language in Thought and Action*, New York: Harcourt, Brace, 1939.
Heider, Fritz, *The Psychology of Interpersonal Relations*, New York: Wiley, 1958.
Herzberg, Frederick, et al., *The Motivation to Work*, New York: Wiley, 1959.
Hixson, Richard F., *Mass Media: A Casebook*, New York: Crowell, 1973.
Holzner, Burkart, *Reality Construction in Society*, Cambridge, Mass.: Schenkman, 1968.
Homans, G. C., *The Human Group*, New York: Harcourt, Brace, 1950.
Innis, Harold A., *The Bias of Communication*, Toronto: University of Toronto Press, 1951.
Jandt, Fred E., *The Process of Interpersonal Communication*, San Francisco: Canfield Press, 1976.
Johnson, David W., *Reaching Out*, Englewood Cliffs, N.J.: Prentice-Hall, 1972.
Johnson, Kenneth G., John J. Senatore, Mark C. Liebig, and Gene Minor, *Nothing Never Happens*, Beverly Hills, Calif.: Glencoe, 1974.
Johnson, Wendell, *People in Quandaries*, New York: Harper, 1946.
Jones, John E. and J. William Pfeiffer, *A Handbook of Structured Experiences in Human Relations Training*, Vol. I–IV, La Jolla, Calif.: University Associates, 1969–1974.
Jourard, Sidney, *The Transparent Self*, New York: Van Nostrand Reinhold, 1968.
Katz, Elihu and Paul F. Lazarsfeld, *Personal Influence*, New York: Free Press, 1955.
Keltner, John W., *Interpersonal Speech-Communication*, Belmont, Calif.: Wadsworth, 1970.
Kibler, Robert J., and Larry L. Barker, *Conceptual Frontiers in Speech*, New York: Speech Association of America, 1969.
Klapper, Joseph T., *The Effects of Mass Communication*, Glencoe, Ill.: Free Press, 1961.
Knapp, Mark L., *Nonverbal Communication in Human Interaction*, New York: Holt, Rinehart and Winston, 1972.
Korzybski, Alfred, *Science and Sanity*, Lakeville, Conn.: The International Non-Aristotelian Library Publishing Company, 1948.
Krupar, Karen R., *Communication Games*, New York: Free Press, 1973.
Lacy, Dan M., *Freedom and Communications*, Urbana: University of Illinois Press, 1965.
Laing, R. D., H. Phillipson, and A. R. Lee, *Interpersonal Perception*, New York: Springer, 1966.
Laing, R. D., *The Politics of Experience*, London: Penguin Books, 1967.

Lakin, M., *Interpersonal Encounter*, New York: McGraw-Hill, 1972.
Leathers, Dale G., *Nonverbal Communication Systems*, Boston: Allyn and Bacon, 1976.
Lederman, Linda C., *New Dimensions: An Introduction to Human Communication*, Dubuque, Iowa: W. C. Brown, 1976.
Lifton, Walter M., *Working with Groups*, New York: Wiley, 1961.
Lingwood, David Alfred, *Interpersonal Communication*, Ann Arbor, Mich.: University Microfilm, 1970.
Luft, Joseph, *Group Processes*, Palo Alto, Calif.: National Press, 1963.
Machlup, Fritz, *The Production and Distribution of Knowledge in the United States*, Princeton, N.J.: Princeton University Press, 1962.
Mann, Richard D., in collaboration with Graham S. Gibbard and John J. Hartman, *Interpersonal Style and Group Development*, New York: Wiley, 1967.
Markham, James W., *International Communication as a Field of Study*, Iowa City, Iowa: International Communication Division, Association for Education in Journalism, 1970.
Matson, Floyd and Ashley Montagu, *The Human Dialogue*, New York: Free Press, 1967.
McCroskey, James and Lawrence R. Wheeless, *Introduction to Human Communication*, Boston: Allyn and Bacon, 1976.
McCroskey, James C., Carl E. Larson and Mark L. Knapp, *An Introduction to Interpersonal Communication*, Englewood Cliffs, N.J.: Prentice-Hall, 1971.
McLuhan, Marshall and Quentin Fiore, *The Medium is the Message*, New York: Random House, 1967.
McLuhan, Marshall, *Understanding Media: The Extensions of Man*, New York: McGraw-Hill, 1964.
McPhee, William N., *Formal Theories of Mass Behavior*, New York: Free Press, 1963.
Mehrabian, Albert, *Non-Verbal Communication*, Chicago: Aldine, 1972.
Mehrabian, Albert, *Silent Messages*, Belmont Calif.: Wadsworth, 1967.
Mendelbaum, Seymour J., *Community and Communications*, New York: W. W. Norton, 1972.
Merrill, John C. and Ralph L. Lowenstein, *Media, Messages and Men*, New York: David McKay, 1971.
Merton, Robert K., *Social Theory and Social Structure*, New York: Free Press, 1957.
Millar, Dan P. and Frank E. Millar, *Message and Myths*, New York: Alfred, 1976.
Miller, George A., *Communication and Language*, New York: Basic Books, 1967.
Miller, George A., *Language and Communication*, New York: McGraw-Hill, 1951.

Miller, Gerald R. and Mark Steinberg, *Between People,* Chicago: Science Research Associates, 1975.

Miller, Gerald R. and Michael Burgoon, *New Techniques in Persuasion,* New York: Harper and Row, 1972.

Morris, Charles, *Signs, Language and Behavior,* New York: Braziller, 1946.

Mortensen, C. David, *Basic Readings in Communication Theory,* New York: Harper and Row, 1973.

Mortensen, C. David, *Communication: The Study of Human Interaction,* New York: McGraw-Hill, 1972.

Myers, Gail E. and Michele Tolela Myers, *The Dynamics of Human Communication: A Laboratory Approach,* New York: McGraw-Hill, 1973.

Nafziger, Ralph O. and David M. White, *Introduction to Mass Communications Research,* Baton Rouge: Louisiana State University Press, 1958.

Olmsted, Michael S., *The Small Group,* New York: Random House, 1959.

Parry, John, *Psychology of Human Communication,* New York: American Elsevier, 1968.

Peterson, Theodore, Jay W. Jensen, and William L. Riverts, *The Mass Media and Modern Society,* New York: Holt, Rinehart, and Winston, 1965.

Phillips, Gerald M., *Communication and the Small Group,* Indianapolis: Bobbs-Merrill, 1966.

Phillips, Gerald M. and Eugene C. Erikson, *Interpersonal Dynamics in the Small Group,* New York: Random House, 1970.

Phillips, Gerald M. and Nancy G. Metzger, *Intimate Communication,* Boston: Allyn and Bacon, 1976.

Pierce, J. R., *Symbols, Signals, and Noise,* New York: Harper and Row, Torchbooks, 1961.

Pike, Kenneth L., *Language in Relation to a Unified Theory of the Structure of Human Behavior,* The Hague: Mouton, 1967.

Richardson, Lee, *Dimensions of Communication,* New York: Appleton-Century-Crofts, 1969.

Rivers, William L. and Wilbur Schramm, *Responsibility in Mass Communication,* New York: Harper and Row, 1969.

Rogers, Carl, *On Becoming a Person,* Boston: Houghton Mifflin, 1961.

Rogers, Everett M., *Communication of Innovations,* New York: Free Press, 1971.

Rosenberg, B. and David M. White, *Mass Culture Revisited,* New York: Van Nostrand, 1971.

Rosenblith, Walter A., *Sensory Communication,* Cambridge: M.I.T. Press, 1961.

Rosenfield, Lawrence, Laurie Hayes, and Thomas Frenz, *The Communicative Experience,* Boston: Allyn and Bacon, 1976.

Roslansky, John D., *Communication,* New York: Fleet Press, 1969.

Ruben, Brent D. and John Y. Kim, *Human Communication and General Systems Theory,* Rochelle Park, N.J.: Hayden, 1975.

Ruben, Brent D. and Richard W. Budd, *Human Communication Handbook: Simulations and Games,* Rochelle Park, N.J.: Hayden, 1975.

Ruesch, Jurgen and Gregory Bateson, *Communication: The Social Matrix of Psychiatry,* New York: W. W. Norton, 1951, 1968.

Ruesch, Jurgen, *Disturbed Communication,* New York: Norton, 1957.

Reusch, Jurgen and Weldon Kees, *Nonverbal Communication,* Berkeley, Calif.: University of California Press, 1956, 1972.

Reusch, Jurgen, *Therapeutic Communication,* New York: Norton, 1961.

Sackman, H. and Norman Nie, *The Information Utility and Social Choice,* Montvale, N.J.: American Federation of Information Processing Societies Press, 1970.

Samovar, Larry A. and Richard E. Porter, *Intercultural Communication,* Belmont, Calif.: Wadsworth, 1976.

Schein, Edgar H. and Warren G. Bennis, *Personal and Organizational Change Through Group Methods,* New York: Wiley, 1965.

Schiller, Herbert I., *Mass Communications and the American Empire,* New York: Augustus Kelley, 1969.

Schramm, Wilbur, *Mass Communications,* Urbana, University of Illinois Press, 1960.

Schramm, Wilbur, *Mass Media and National Development,* Stanford: Stanford University Press, 1964.

Schramm, Wilbur, *Responsibility in Mass Communication,* New York: Harper, 1957.

Schramm, Wilbur, *The Process and Effects of Mass Communication,* Urbana: University of Illinois Press, 1954.

Schramm, Wilbur, *The Science of Human Communication,* New York: Basic Books, 1963.

Schroder, H. M., M. J. Driver and S. Steufert, *Human Information Processing,* New York: Holt, Rinehart and Winston, 1967.

Sereno, Kenneth K. and C. David Mortensen (eds.), *Foundations of Communication Theory,* New York: Harper, 1970.

Sereno, Kenneth K. and Edward M. Bodaken, *Trans-Per: Understanding Human Communication,* Boston: Houghton Mifflin, 1975.

Shands, Harley, *Thinking and Psychotherapy,* Cambridge, Mass.: Harvard University Press, 1960.

Sherif, Muzafer and Carl I. Hovland, *Social Judgment,* New Haven: Yale University Press, 1961.

Shibutani, Tamotsu, *Society and Personality,* Englewood Cliffs, N.J.: Prentice-Hall, 1961.

Siebert, Frederick, Theodore Peterson and Wilbur Schramm, *Four Theories of the Press,* Urbana: University of Illinois Press, 1956.

Smith, Alfred G., *Communication and Culture,* New York: Holt, Rinehart and Winston, 1966.

Sommer, R., *Personal Space,* Englewood Cliffs, N.J.: Prentice-Hall, 1969.

Stewart, Daniel K., *The Psychology of Communication*, New York: Funk and Wagnalls, 1969.
Tepper, Albert and Paul Roman, *Oral Communication*, Minneapolis, Minnesota: Burgess Publishing, 1968.
Thayer, Lee, *Communication and Communication Systems*, Homewood, Ill.: Richard D. Irwin, 1968.
Tiger, Lionel, *Men in Groups*, New York: Random House, Vintage Books, 1969.
Tompkins, Charles, *Concepts of Communication*, New York: Wiley, 1971.
Vickers, Geoffrey, *Value Systems and Social Process*, New York: Basic Books, 1968.
Vickers, G., *The Art of Judgment*, London: Chapman-Hall, 1965.
Watson, O. M., *Proxemic Behavior*, The Hague: Mouton, 1970.
Watzlawick, Paul, Janet H. Beavin, and Don D. Jackson, *Pragmatics of Human Communication*, New York: W. W. Norton & Company, 1967.
Weaver, Carl H., *Human Listening*, Indianapolis, Indiana: Bobbs-Merrill, 1972.
Whorf, B. L., *Language, Thought, and Reality*, Cambridge, Mass.: M.I.T. Press, 1956.
Weiner, N., *The Human Use of Human Beings*, New York: Avon, 1950.

Readings in Experience-Based Learning Theory

Abt, Clark, "Education is Child's Play," in Werner Z. Hirsch et al., *Inventing Education for the Future*, San Francisco: Chandler Publishing Co., 1967.
Archambault, Reginald, *Lectures in the Philosophy of Education: 1899 by John Dewey*, New York: Random House, 1966.
Boocock, Sarane S., "Instructional Games," in *Encyclopedia of Education*, New York: Macmillan Company, 1971.
Boocock, Sarane S., *Simulation Games in Learning*, Beverly Hills, Calif.: Sage Publications, 1968.
Bruner, J. S., *Learning About Learning: A Conference Report*, Washington: U.S. Government Printing Office, 1966.
Bruner, J. S., *The Process of Education*, Cambridge, Mass.: Harvard Press, 1961.
Bruner, J. S., *The Relevance of Education*, New York: Norton, 1971.
Bruner, J. S., *Toward a Theory of Instruction*, New York: Norton, 1966.
Bruner, J. S., Rose R. Oliver and Patricia M. Greenfield, *et al.*, *Studies in Cognitive Growth*, New York: Wiley, 1966.
Budd, Richard W., "Communication, Education and Simulation: Some Thoughts on the Learning Process," Institute for Communication Studies, Rutgers University, 1970.
Budd, Richard W., "The Impact of the Mass Media on Curricula," in Richard W. Burns and Gary D. Brooks, eds., *Curriculum Design in a Changing Society*, Englewood Cliffs, N.J.: Educational Technology Press, 1972.

Carlson, Elliot, "Games in the Classroom," *Saturday Review:* April 15, 1967.
Coleman, James S., "Social Processes and Social Simulation Games," in Boocock and Schild, eds., *Simulation Games in Learning,* Beverly Hills, Calif.: Sage Publications, 1968.
Danish, Paul, *Champaign Report: A Conference on Educational Reform—A Student View,* Champaign, Ill., September, 1966.
Dewey, John, *Experience and Education,* New York: Macmillan, 1938.
Duke, Richard D., *Gaming: A Future's Language,* Beverly Hills, Calif.: Sage Publications, Inc., 1974.
Gardner, John W., *Self-Renewal: The Individual and the Innovative Society,* New York: Harper & Row, 1965.
Gordon, Alice Kaplan, *Games for Growth,* Palo Alto, Calif.: Science Research Associates, 1970.
Greenblat, Cathy S., "Gaming as Applied Sociology," in Arthur Shostak, ed., *Putting Sociology to Work,* New York: David McKay, 1974.
Greenblat, Cathy S. and Richard D. Duke, eds., *Gaming-Simulation,* New York: John Wiley, 1975.
Harvey, O. J., *Experience, Structure and Adaptability,* New York: Springer, 1966.
Montessori, Maria, *Spontaneous Activity in Education,* New York: Schocken, 1965.
Neill, A. S., *Summerhill: A Radical Approach to Child Rearing,* New York: Hart, 1960.
Postman, Neil and Charles Weingartner, *Teaching as a Subversive Activity,* New York: Delacorte, 1969.
Riesman, David, *Constraint and Variety of American Education,* Lincoln, Nebr.: University of Nebraska Press, 1968.
Rogers, Carl R., *Freedom to Learn,* Columbus, Ohio: Charles E. Merrill, 1969.
Ruben, Brent D., *Interact,* Kennebunkport, Maine: Mercer House Press, 1973.
Ruben, Brent D., "The What and Why of Gaming: A Taxonomy of Experiential Learning Systems," in *Proceedings 1973* of the Annual Symposium of The National Gaming Council and the International Simulation and Gaming Association, Gaithersburg, Maryland, 1973.
Ruben, Brent D. and Richard W. Budd, *Human Communication Handbook: Simulations and Games,* Rochelle Park, N.J.: Hayden, 1975.
Schroder, Harold M., Michael J. Driver and Siegfried Streufert, *Human Information Processing,* New York: Holt, Rinehart and Winston, 1967.
Shirts, R. Garry, "Games Students Play," *Saturday Review:* May 16, 1970.
Shulman, Lee S. and Evan R. Keisler, ed., *Learning by Discovery: A Critical Appraisal,* Chicago: Rand McNally, 1966.
Suits, Bernard, "What is a Game?" *Philosophy of Science:* June, 1967.
Thayer, Lee, "On Communication and Change: Some Provocations, *Systematics,* Vol. 6, No. 3, December, 1968.
Upton, Albert, *Design for Thinking,* Stanford: Stanford University Press, 1961.

Readings in Institutional Simulations and Games

Abt, Clark C., *Serious Games,* New York: Viking, 1970.

Armstrong, R. H. R. and R. J. Taylor, *Instructional Simulation Systems in Higher Education,* Cambridge, Mass.: Cambridge University Press, 1970.

Attig, J. C., "Use of Games as a Teaching Technique," in *Social Studies*, Vol. 58, January, 1967.

Boocock, Sarane S., "Games Change What Goes on in the Classroom," in *Nation's Schools,* Vol. 80, October, 1967.

Boocock, Sarane S., "Instructional Games," in *Encyclopedia of Education*, New York: Macmillan, 1971.

Boocock, Sarane S. and James S. Coleman, "Games with Simulated Environments in Learning," in *Sociology of Education,* Vol. 39, Summer, 1966.

Boocock, Sarane S. and E. O. Schild, eds., *Simulation Games in Learning,* Beverly Hills, Calif.: Sage, 1971.

Brodbelt, Samuel, "Simulation in the Social Studies: An Overview," *Social Education* Vol. 33, February, 1969.

Burgess, Philip, "Organizing Simulated Environments," in *Social Education,* Vol. 33, February, 1969.

Carlson, Elliot, *Learning through Games,* Washington, D.C.: Public Affairs Press, 1969.

Cherryholmes, Cleo H., "Some Current Research on Effectiveness of Educational Simulations: Implications for Alternative Strategies," in *American Behavioral Scientist,* Vol. X, No. 2, October, 1966.

Cohen, B. C., "Political Gaming in the Classroom," *Journal of Politics,* Vol. 24, May, 1962.

Cohen, Kalman J. and Eric Rhenman, "The Role of Management Games in Education and Research," in *Management Science,* Vol. 7, 1961.

Coleman, James S., "Games as Vehicles for Social Theory," in *American Behavioral Scientist,* Vol. 12, July–August, 1969.

Coleman, James S., "Learning Through Games," in *NEA Journal,* Vol. 56, January, 1967.

Coleman, James S., "Simulation Games and Social Theory," Baltimore Md.: Center for the Study of Social Organization of Schools, Johns Hopkins University, Report No. 8, 1968 (mimeo).

Crawford, Meredith P., "Dimensions of Simulation," in *American Psychologist,* Vol. 21, No. 8, August, 1966.

Cruickshank, D. R., "The Use of Simulation in Teacher Education: A Developing Phenomenon," *Journal of Teacher Education,* Vol. 20, Spring, 1970.

Dill, William R. and Neil Doppelt, "The Acquisition of Experience in Complex Management Game," in *Management Science,* Vol. 10, No. 1, October, 1963.

Druckman, Daniel, "Understanding the Operation of Complex Social Systems: Some Uses of Simulation Design," *Simulation and Games,* Vol. 2, June, 1971.

Edwards, Keith J., "The Effect of Ability, Achievement, and Number of Plays on Learning from a Simulation Game," Baltimore: Center for Social Organization of Schools, The Johns Hopkins University Report No. 115, 1971.

Fennessey, Gail M., Samuel A. Livingston, Keith J. Edwards, Steven J. Kidder, Alyce W. Nafziger, "Simulation, Gaming and Conventional Instruction: An Experimental Comparison," Baltimore: Center for Social Organization of Schools, The Johns Hopkins University, Report No. 128, 1972.

Fletcher, Jerry L., "The Effectiveness of Simulation Games as Learning Environments: A Proposed Program of Research," in *Simulation and Games,* Vol. 2, December, 1971.

Fletcher, Jerry L., "Evaluation of Learning in Two Social Studies Simulation Games," in *Simulation and Games,* Vol. 2, September, 1971.

Gamson, William A., "SIMSOC: Establishing Social Order in a Simulated Society," in *Simulation and Games,* Vol. 2, September, 1971.

Goodman, Fred L., "Games and Simulations," in Robert Travers, ed., *Handbook of Research on Teaching,* 2nd ed., Chicago: Rand McNally, 1972.

Gordon, Alice Kaplan, *Games for Growth,* Palo Alto, Calif.: Science Research Associates, 1970.

Greenblat, Cathy S., "Gaming and Simulation in the Social Sciences," in *A Guide to the Literature,* New Brunswick, N.J.: Douglass College, Rutgers University, 1972.

Greenblatt, Cathy S., "Simulations, Games and the Sociologist," in *The American Sociologist,* Vol. 6, May, 1971.

Greenblat, Cathy S., "Teaching with Simulation Games: A Review of Claims and Evidence," in *Teaching Sociology,* Vol. 1, October, 1972.

Greenblat, Cathy S. and Richard D. Duke, eds., *Gaming-Simulation,* New York: John Wiley, 1975.

Grove, Theodore G., *Experiences in Interpersonal Communication,* Englewood Cliffs, N.J.: Prentice-Hall, 1976.

Hearn, Edell M. and Thomas Reddick, *Simulated Behavioral Teaching Situations,* Dubuque, Iowa: W. C. Brown, 1971.

Inbar, Michael, "Participating in a Simulation Game," in *The Journal of Applied Behavioral Science,* Vol. 6, 1970.

Inbar, Michael and C. S. Stoll, eds., *Simulation and Gaming in Social Science,* New York: Free Press, 1972.

Johnson, David W., *Reaching Out,* Englewood Cliffs, N.J.: Prentice-Hall, 1972.

Johnson, Kenneth G., John J. Senatore, Mark C. Liebig, and Gene Minor, *Nothing Never Happens,* Beverly Hills, Calif.: Glencoe, 1974.

Jones, John E. and J. William Pfeiffer, *A Handbook of Structured Experiences in Human Relations Training,* Vol. I–IV, La Jolla, Calif.: University Associates, 1969–1974.

Kasperson, Roger E., "Games as Educational Media," in *Journal of Geography,* Vol. 62, October, 1968.

Kidder, Steven J., *Simulation Games: Practical References, Potential Use, Selected Bibliography,* Baltimore, Md.: Center for Social Organization of Schools, Johns Hopkins University, 1971.

Kidder, Steven J., "Emotional Arousal and Attitude Change During Simulation Games," Baltimore: Center of Social Organization of Schools, The Johns Hopkins University, Report No. 111, 1971.

Kidder, Steven J. and John T. Guthrie, "Training Effects of a Behavior Modification Game," *Stimulation and Games,* Vol. 3, March, 1972.

Klietsch, Ronald, *An Introduction to Learning Games and Instructional Simulations,* St. Paul, Minn.: Instructional Simulations, 1969.

Klietsch, Ronald and Fred Wiegman, *Directory of Educational Simulations, Learning Games, and Didactic Units,* St. Paul, Minn.: Instructional Simulations, 1969.

Kraft, Ivor, "Pedagogical Futility in Fun and Games," *National Education Association Journal,* Vol. 56, January, 1967.

Krupar, Karen R., *Communication Games,* New York: Free Press, 1973.

Lederman, Linda C., *New Dimensions: An Introduction to Human Communication,* Dubuque, Iowa: Wm. C. Brown, 1976.

Livingston, Samuel A. and Clarence S. Stoll, *Simulation Games for the Social Studies Teacher,* New York: Free Press, 1973.

MacLean, Malcolm S., Jr., "Theory, Method and Games in Communication," in *Mass Media and International Understanding,* France Vreg, ed., Ljubljana, Yugoslavia: School of Sociology, Political Science and Journalism, Part I, 1969.

MacLean, Malcolm S., Jr. and Albert D. Talbott, "Approaches to Speech-Communication Theory Through Simulation and Games," paper presented at the Speech Association of American/International Communication Association Annual Meeting, New York City, December, 1969.

McKenney, James and William R. Dill, "Influences on Learning in Simulation Games," in *American Behavioral Scientist,* Vol. 10, October, 1966.

Myers, Gail E. and Michele Tolela Myers, *The Dynamics of Human Communication: A Laboratory Approach,* New York: McGraw-Hill, 1973.

Nesbitt, William, *Simulation Games for the Social Studies Classroom,* New York: Crowell, 1971 (Revised Edition).

Pitts, Forrest, *The Varieties of Simulation: A Review and Bibliography,* Philadelphia: Regional Science Research Institute.

Ramey, James W., "Simulation in Library Administration," *Journal of Education for Librarianship:* Vol. VIII, Fall, 1967.

Raser, John R., *Simulation and Society: An Exploration of Scientific Gaming,* Boston: Allyn and Bacon, 1969.

Raser, John R., Donald T. Campbell and Richard W. Chadwick, "Gaming and Simulation for Developing Theory Relevant to International Relations," in *General Systems,* Ludwig von Bertalanffy and Anatol Rapoport, eds., Washington, D.C.: Society for General Systems Research, 1970.

Robinson, James, "Simulation and Games," in *The New Media and Education*, Peter Rossi and Bruce Biddle, eds., Chicago: Aldine, 1966.

Ruben, Brent D., *Interact*, Kennebunkport, Maine: Mercer House Press, 1973.

Ruben, Brent D., "The What and Why of Gaming: A Taxonomy of Experiential Learning Systems," in *Proceedings 1973* of the Annual Symposium of The National Gaming Council and the International Simulation and Gaming Association, Gaithersburg, Maryland, 1973.

Ruben, Brent D. and Albert D. Talbott, "The Communication System Simulation: An Overview," Iowa City, Iowa: University of Iowa, January, 1970. (mimeo)

Ruben, Brent D., Albert D. Talbott, Lee M. Brown and Henry G. LaBrie, *Intermedia: Participant's Manual*, Iowa City, Iowa: University Associates Press, 1970.

Ruben, B. R., "Games and Simulations: Materials, Sources, and Learning Concepts," in J. W. Pfeiffer and J. E. Jones, eds., *The 1972 Annual Handbook for Group Facilitators*, La Jolla, Calif.: University Associates Press, 1972.

Ruben, Brent D. and Richard W. Budd, *Human Communication Handbook: Simulations and Games*, Rochelle Park, N.J.: Hayden, 1975.

Russell, Constance J., "Simulating the Adolescent Society: A Validity Study," *Simulations and Games*, Vol. 3, June, 1972.

"Selective Bibliography on Simulation Games as Learning Devices" in *American Behavioral Scientist*, Vol. 10, November, 1966.

Stoll, Clarice S. and Michael Inbar, "Games and Socialization: An Exploratory Study of Race Differences," *Sociological Quarterly*, Vol. 2, Summer, 1970.

Talbott, Albert D. and Brent D. Ruben, *Communication System Simulation Participant's Manual*, Iowa City, Iowa: University of Iowa, School of Journalism, 1970. (mimeo)

Tansey, P. J., ed., *Education Aspects of Simulation*, Maidenhead, England: McGraw-Hill, 1971.

Tansey, P. J. "Simulation Techniques in the Training of Teachers," in *Simulation and Games*, Vol. 1, September, 1970.

Tansey, P. J. and D. Unwin, *Simulation and Gaming in Education*, London: Methuen, and New York: Barnes and Noble, 1969.

Taylor, John L. and Rex Walford, *Simulation in the Classroom*, Baltimore: Penguin, 1972.

Thayer, Lee, *Studies in the Development of Administrators: II An Experimental Training Program*, Wichita, Kansas: College of Business Administration, Wichita State University, 1964.

Twelker, Paul A., ed., *Instructional Simulation Systems*, Corvallis, Ore.: Continuing Education Publications, Oregon State University, Department of Printing, 1969.

Twelker, Paul A., "Designing Simulation Systems," *Educational Technology:* October, 1969.

Twelker, Paul A., "Some Reflections on Instructional Simulation and Gaming," *Simulations and Games,* Vol. 3, June, 1972.
Walford, R., *Games in Geography,* London: Longmans, 1969.
Werner, Roland and Joan T. Werner, *Bibliography of Simulations, Social Systems and Education,* LaJolla, Calif.: Western Behavioral Sciences Institute, 1969.
Wilson, J. P. and D. E. Adams, "A Selected Bibliography of Simulation and Related Subject, 1960-1969," Pittsburg, Kansas: Political Science, Kansas State College, April 6, 1970.
Youngers, John C. and John F. Aceti, *Simulation Games and Activities for Social Studies,* Dansville, N.Y.: The Instructor Publications, 1969.
Zieler, Richard, *Games for School Use: An Annotated List,* Yorktown Heights, N.Y.: Board of Cooperative Educational Services.
Zuckerman, David W. and Robert E. Horn, *The Guide to Simulation Games for Education and Training,* Cambridge, Mass.: Information Resources, 1970.

Readings in Instructional Role Playing and Structured Exercises

Bavelas, Alex, "Role Playing and Management Training," *Sociatry,* Vol. 1, No. 2, June 1947.
Blansfield, Michael G., "Role-Playing as a Method in Executive Development," *Personnel Journal,* Vol. 34, 1953.
Chesler, Mark and Robert Fox, *Role-Playing Methods in the Classroom,* Chicago: Science Research Associates, 1966.
Corsini, Raymond J., Malcolm E. Shaw and Robert R. Blake, *Roleplaying in Business and Industry,* New York: Free Press, 1961.
Elms, Alan C., *Role Playing, Reward and Attitude Change,* New York: Van Nostrand-Reinhold, 1971.
Garvey, Dale M., *Simulation, Role Playing and Socio-Drama in the Social Studies,* Emporia, Kansas: Emporia State Research Studies, 1967.
Lowell, Mildred H., *Role Playing and Other Management Cases,* Metuchen, N.J.: Scarecrow, 1971.
Mann, John H., "Experimental Evaluations of Role Playing," *Psychological Bulletin,* Vol. 53, No. 3, May, 1956.
Mial, Dorothy J. and Stanley Jacobson, "10 Interaction Exercises for the Classroom," Washington: National Training Laboratory, Institute for Applied Behavioral Science.
Moreno, J. L., *Psychodrama,* Vol. 1, New York: Beacon, 1946.
Nylen, Donald J., Robert Mitchell and Anthony Stout, *Handbook of Staff Development and Human Relations Training: Materials Developed for Use in Africa,* Washington: National Training Laboratory, Institute for Applied Behavioral Science, 1967.
Parnes, Sidney J., *Creative Behavior Guidebook,* New York: Scribner's, 1967.
Parnes, Sidney J., *Creative Behavior Workbook,* New York: Scribner's, 1967.
Pfeiffer, J. William and John E. Jones, *A Handbook of Structured Experiences*

for Human Relations Training, Volumes I-VI, La Jolla, Calif.: University Associates, 1969-1976.

Pfeiffer, J. William and John E. Jones, *The Annual Handbook for Group Facilitators,* La Jolla, Calif.: University Associates Press, 1972-1976.

Scher, Jordan M., "Two Disruptions of the Communication Zone: A Discussion of Action and Role Playing Techniques," *Group Psychotherapy,* Vol. XII, No. 2, June, 1959.

Shaftel, Fannie R., *Role-Playing for Social Values: Decision-Making in The Social Studies,* Englewood Cliffs, N.J.: Prentice-Hall, 1967.

PART 1.

INTRAPERSONAL COMMUNICATION

If communication is one of the two essential life processes of all living things,[1] *intrapersonal communication*—sensing, making sense of, and acting toward one's environment—occupies a central role in the study of human behavior. Serving sometimes as a communicator, initiator, or mass communicator of messages; sometimes as a recipient, receiver or audience member; and often more or less simultaneously as both, the *individual,* and the intrapersonal communication dynamic is clearly at the center of the communication process. It is through personal communication processes that humans develop, maintain, or change their images of their environments and the people and things which compose them. And it is based upon the meanings that people have for these objects and persons, that they behave.[2]

These personalized "maps" for *understanding* and *acting* toward the environment begin to take shape from the moment of birth—perhaps well before—as the child experiences the environment and strives to understanding it. Most scholars view this communicational adaptation process as an active one. The individual is not seen as a passive recipient of stimuli or messages which program him or her in a particular way. Rather the person is viewed as a *selective agent,* "picking and choosing" the messages he or she will attend to and the meanings to attach to those messages, on the basis of needs, values, goals, and aspirations, as well as past experience.

It is a common assumption that people select and interpret the same things in the same way. And while it might often appear as if people are, in fact, *communicated-with,* and to some extent also *communicate-to* others in more or less the same way, this proposition often turns out to be misleading. It is indeed seldom when the messages attended to and interpretations of two or more individuals closely correspond. To note that we buy different cars, appreciate different perfumes, read different newspapers and magazines, enjoy different television programs, select different mates, choose different friends, political parties, life styles, vocations, and avocations is to cite only the most obvious evidence that different persons attach different meanings to different objects, persons, and events in their environment.

The more one recognizes the significance of such interpretative differences to the conduct of human affairs, the more importance one attaches to human communication—and the process by which these ways of relating to one's environment are generated, integrated, maintained, or changed.

It is not impossible to intellectually grasp the notion that there are important, non-transitory differences between people in terms of how they select and interpret the messages around them. But while the idea can be comprehended *in theory*, it is extremely difficult to integrate and apply to one's own behavior, *in practice*. How often are we surprised, shocked, or frustrated to find that an acquaintance, friend, or associate assumes that we meant one thing by a message, and *we knew* we meant something quite different? Too often, even those of us who may spend our lifetimes studying communication and human behavior, find ourselves behaving as if our understandings or interpretations were *the right, true* or *appropriate ones*. It goes almost without saying, that to the extent we fall victim to this communication malady, we close ourselves off from the very information and persons we need in order to grow or change.

From a pragmatic perspective, it is also important to keep in mind that one's effectiveness as a communicator can be measured only in terms of the intended audience one has for his or her messages, and in terms of their responses to our intentions. To the extent that one is unaware or unconcerned with the responses of other people, he or she will be successful as a communicator only on a random basis. It is probably a recognition of this complex state of affairs that led to the authoring of the increasingly popular phrase:

I Know You Believe You Understand What You Think I Said, But I am Sure You Realize That What You Heard Is Not What I Meant.

The activities in this section of the book deal directly with aspects of the personal communication process, focusing both on the dynamics of *communicating-to* and *being communicated-with*. In general the intent is to heighten participant awareness of how intrapersonal processes operate and of the role each individual plays in communication outcomes. The activities include focus on personal communication behavior, experience, attention, and memory; assumptions, context, and expectations; values, decision-making, meaning and category formation, perceptual patterning, language and meaning, message response set, observation and inference, listening, and listening-response set.

References

1. *Cf.* James G. Miller, "Living Systems," *Behavioral Science,* Vol. 10, 1965; Lee Thayer, *Communication and Communication Systems,* Homewood, Ill.: Irwin, 1968; Brent D. Ruben, "General System Theory; An Approach to Human Communication," in *Approaches to Human Communication,"*; R. W. Budd and B. D. Ruben, (eds.), Rochelle Park, N.J.: Hayden, 1972; and Brent D. Ruben and John Y. Kim, *General Systems Theory and Human Communication,* Rochelle Park, N.J.: Hayden, 1975.
2. *Cf.* Herbert Blumer, *Symbolic Interactionism,* Englewood Cliffs: N.J.: Prentice-Hall, 1969, and "Symbolic Interaction: An Approach to Human Communication," in *Approaches to Human Communication,* R. W. Budd and B. D. Ruben, *op. cit.*

1. Communication Inventory

The inventory is designed to facilitate the systematic identification of an individual's communication behaviors. With a series of directed questions the exercise guides the individual through an assessment of the range and extent of mass media use and interpersonal networks.

Procedure

1. Participants are each provided a copy of the questionnaire shown in Worksheet 1.1.
2. After necessary clarifications, participants are told to keep a record of the particular behaviors to which the form refers, over a period of several days to a week. (At the discretion of the instructor/facilitator.)
3. At the end of the recording period, participants tabulate their records and complete the questionnaire.
4. The completed individual profiles can be utilized as the basis for group discussion aimed at increasing individual awareness of their own and others communication behaviors.
5. Another option is to collect the profiles for a more rigorous analysis; individuals can later be provided with data on how their communication behaviors were similar to and different from those of other group members, or previous comparable groups.

Worksheet 1.1

COMMUNICATION BEHAVIOR INVENTORY

I. Media Use Profile

1. How many hours a day do you:
   (a) listen to the radio?
   (b) watch TV?
   (c) listen to tapes or records?
   (d) read newspapers?
   (e) read magazines?
   (f) read required books?
   (g) read non-required books?
2. In order of your listening preference, list the radio stations you listen to regularly.
3. List all the TV shows you watch regularly.
4. How many movies (non-TV) do you see a month?
5. List the last 5 movies you've seen.
6. How often a year do you:
   (a) see a play?
   (b) go to the opera?
   (c) see a dance company?
   (d) go to an art exhibit?
   (e) go to a museum?

7. How many records and/or tapes do you own?
8. How many records or tapes do you buy each month?
9. Which records or tapes do you play most frequently?
10. List the newspapers you read regularly.
11. What magazines do you subscribe to or read regularly?
12. List the "non-assigned" books you've read in the last 6 months.

II. Interpersonal Profile

13. List those persons you call on the phone regularly
14. How often do you call them each week?
15. List those who call you on the phone regularly?
16. How often do they call each week?
17. How many items of mail do you receive each week?
    (a) addressed to you?
    (b) addressed to occupant?
18. How many letters do you send each week?
19. To whom do you send letters?
20. List the places you eat your meals.
21. How many people do you usually eat with?
22. Who are they?
23. List the places where you study.
24. How many people do you usually study with?
25. Who are they?
26. How many of those listed in answer to question 25 are different from those listed in answer to question 22?
27. Where do you spend your social and recreational time? (List the places.)
28. Who are the people normally involved in these activities with you?
29. How many of these people do not appear in answers to either No. 22. or No. 26?
30. Do you have a job?
31. Who do you talk with at work?
32. Do you ever see these individuals outside of work?
33. How often?
34. Do you do volunteer work?
35. Who do you talk with in the volunteer context?
36. Do you ever socialize with those individuals in a different context?
37. What other activities are you involved with?
38. With whom do you interact while involved in these activities?
39. Do you own a citizen band (CB) radio?
40. If so, how many hours a week do you use it?
41. If you use a CB, how many different persons do you regularly talk to?

2. Experience, Attention, and Memory

This memory game focuses upon intrapersonal information processing, and upon experience, attention and memory. The activity requires approximately 1 hour and can be most appropriately used with 20-40 participants.

Procedure

1. The instructor assembles a number of objects and arranges them on a table in front of the room. The table is covered with a sheet or newspaper so that the objects are not visible except at the appropriate times. The items selected for inclusion, and the manner in which they are placed and located relative to one another on the table, will vary somewhat with the purposes of the instructor and the nature of the participants, but generally will include some of the following objects:

    1. rosary
    2. dreidel
    3. worry beads
    4. contact lens case
    5. fountain pen
    6. regular ink pen
    7. ball point pen
    8. pencil
    9. crayon
    10. letter opener
    11. pilot wings
    12. bobbin
    13. guitar pick
    14. thread
    15. cup and saucer
    16. tea bags
    17. fork and spoons
    18. light bulb
    19. *Playgirl* magazine
    20. necklace
    21. battery
    22. flashlight
    23. *Playboy* magazine
    24. *Seventeen* magazine
    25. best selling paperback novel
    26. chalk
    27. safety pin
    28. leather strap
    29. bottle cap
    30. shoe
    31. film
    32. polished stone
    33. money
    34. baseball
    35. eye glasses
    36. cigarettes
    37. matches or lighter
    38. plant
    39. plant mister
    40. towel
    41. hair ribbons
    42. empty beer bottle

2. The objects are symbolically selected to represent a range of activities common to some or all participants. Some of the items have religious associations, some relate to hobbies, others to vocational interests. Some items are common to the daily routines of most participants.
3. A group of 5-7 persons is told to gather around the table, which is still covered with the sheet.
4. The instructor explains that the table contains a number of objects, and that when uncovered participants should strive to remember as many of the

objects as possible, so that when they return to their seats they will be able to list all that they saw.
5. The table is uncovered for approximately 2 minutes, then the sheet is replaced, and participants return to their seats to individually list as many items as they can recall.
6. Another group of 5–7 persons gathers around the table, and the process is repeated until all participants have viewed the items for 2 minutes and returned to compile their individual lists.

Discussion

Because most participants perceive the task as a test of their memory, their attention is focused solely upon striving to recall as many items as possible, often in a competitive effort to do as well as, or better than, other individuals. There are, of course, many more items than anyone can remember, so that in one way or another each individual *selects* from the total possible range of items, some manageable subset he or she will remember. The processes by which these decisions are made—*what to attend to* and *what to recall*—are more or less unconscious. The total recall pattern, however, demonstrates remarkably well to the participant that information processing depends considerably upon experiences and habits. The rosary is most typically listed by someone who is either Catholic or well acquainted with the religion, whereas that same person may not notice or recall the dreidel, a symbol that will be most typically attended to and remembered by a person of the Jewish faith.

Some items will be noticed and recalled mostly by virtue of their *size* or their *placement* on the table. Some participants may notice and recall items which they perceptually *group* with one another as they're noticed, as with cup and saucer, and fork and spoon. If participants are students, such items as books, pens, pencils, etc., are likely to be grouped, noticed, and recalled.

Each person's listing of items then provides the basis for a useful discussion of the dynamics of attention and memory, and the role experience and familiarity play in intrapersonal communication.

How many items were remembered? What factors seem to play a central role in determining whether or not a given item was remembered? Time constraints? Placement? Familiarity to participants? Size? Were particular items remembered by most participants? Which? Why? Were other items only noticed and remembered by a few persons? Which? Why? What role does religious background play in the attention one pays to particular items in the exercise? What is the role of hobbies? Of sex? Of vocation? Of age? Of values? Did any one list items which actually were not present on the table? Which items? How can this be explained? Does one's list indicate anything about the individual who constructed it? Do the lists of remembered items of the entire group have any implications? What relationship does this exercise have to intrapersonal communication processes in everyday life? Does attention normally operate as it did in this activity? Does memory? What are some implications of this exercise for everyday intrapersonal communication processes?

3. Assumptions, Context, Expectations

This activity highlights for discussion the role of assumptions, context, experience, and expectations in intrapersonal communication processes. The exercise may be used with any number of participants and requires approximately 15 minutes to complete.

Procedure

1. The equations shown in Fig. 3.1 are placed one at a time on a flip chart or blackboard.
2. As each equation is displayed, the instructor asks if everyone understands the equation.
3. As equation (**d**) is displayed, participants are likely to indicate that it is incorrect. The instructor reassures them that it is not, and that it follows the same lines of reasoning as the previous equations.
4. Another equation is uncovered, and another, as participants are asked whether they understand the rationale of the equations.
5. The instructor continues until all equations are displayed or until participants indicate that they understand what has been occurring. As necessary, the instructor then explains that the equations represent clock math; ten o'clock plus three hours is one o'clock ($10 + 3 = 1$).

Fig. 3.1

Sample Equations

a. $2 + 2 = 4$
b. $4 + 4 = 8$
c. $5 + 4 = 9$
d. $10 + 3 = 1$
e. $5 + 7 = 12$
f. $11 + 4 = 3$

Discussion

What assumptions were made by participants? How did their expectations influence their responses? What happened when the fourth equation was presented and did not appear to fit the pattern? How difficult or easy was it for participants to consider alternative patterns? How was the problem solved? How did the context of the classroom impact their approach to the equations? How did the form of the equations influence their message set? What aspects of this experience have applicability in normal daily communication situations?

4. Values and Decision-Making

This exercise is designed to focus upon values and their relation to decision-making. The activity requires approximately 30–60 minutes and can be utilized with 5 to 50 participants, alone or in groups.

Procedure

1. Participants are given the incident description, role identities, and instructions provided in Worksheet 4.1.
2. After reading through the introductory material, participants are asked to select the five individuals whom they would place in the hypothetical lifeboat.
3. Groups may be formed with instructions to arrive at a compromise solution with which all group members agree. Or, if small group dynamics are not pertinent to the facilitator's goals, it may be useful to move directly from the selection stage to the facilitated discussion.

Worksheet 4.1

VALUES AND DECISION-MAKING

Consider the Following Problem:

An ocean liner, enroute from Singapore to San Francisco, is destroyed by an explosion. Only twelve people, other than yourself, have managed to reach a lifeboat thrown clear of the blast. The boat is but a transitory haven, however, for it too has been seriously damaged and is leaking badly. Despite feverish bailing and extensive efforts to repair the craft, it is obvious that in a matter of hours it will break apart, sending its passengers to a watery grave. Aboard the boat is an inflatable rubber raft, so small that it will take but five persons. It represents the only chance for escape.

The Captain is the only member of the crew to reach the lifeboat, and he assumes responsibility for the welfare of the other survivors. Although he has decided to go down with the ship, he suggests that the others draw lots to see which five persons will go aboard the rubber raft. Unfortunately, he is over-ruled. In the interests of dispassionate emotions, the twelve have unanimously decided that the Captain choose the five who will be allowed onto the rubber raft.

Which five of the twelve should he select? Explain as fully as you can why he would choose some and not others. A list of the passengers in the lifeboat, together with their personal credentials, follows:

DR. MICHAEL OBERHAUSER ... age 62. A medical doctor with long and selfless service in medicine, specializing in the treatment of cancer. Purportedly on the verge of developing a cure.

REV. ISAAC JOHNSON ... age 33. Black militant minister, a spiritual and political leader of the American Blacks. Although he rejects the use of violence to achieve social parity, he enjoys as strong a following among radicals as he does among moderate Blacks.

Intrapersonal Communication

He was travelling to San Francisco, where he is scheduled to appear before the court to answer charges of illegally using federal funds to sponsor business ventures in the ghetto.

REGINA FOSDICK ... age 32. Successor to Betty Friedan as spokesperson for the Women's Lib movement. As attractive as Gloria Steinem, as bright and articulate as Kate Millet, she is as admired by women in the Movement as is Johnson by Blacks; her philosophical novel, *The Season of Sex*, has been highly praised by critics.

PRESTON CABOT ... age 43. Cabot is a successful banker from New Rochelle, New York, whose record of service to the community is evidenced by his membership in the Rotary Club, Elks, and Lions. He is chairman of the Jaycees, chairman of the New York Republican Party, and founder of a treatment center for alcoholics.

CLAIRE CABOT ... age 24. Pregnant and third wife of Preston, member of New Rochelle Country Club, and organizer of the Bridge Club for harried housewives. Somewhat frustrated in her role as housewife, she has been fighting the temptation of afternoon martini get-togethers at the club.

HANS KREITZER ... age 72. Born "Fyodor Ivanovich Zukov" in the Ukraine, but moved to Germany while very young. After outstanding achievements at various schools and universities, entered field of nuclear physics. Left Germany in 1933, went to England, and later to the USA, where he is considered to be a leading scientist in the area of atomic energy.

MICHAEL WARD ARMSTRONG III ... age 20. Leader of YAF, a college vigilante committee dedicated to cleansing campuses of liberals. He is a protege of an ex-Senator from New York and has been accepted by the Harvard Law School.

LORENZO FALCO ... age 26. Former star pupil of Connie "the gun" Cafferelli, reputed Godfather of the syndicate. Knows the rackets inside and out. He is to testify before a Senate Subcommittee investigating organized crime. What he knows, if made public, should put a crimp in drug traffic.

SAM CARROWAY ... age 38. Unknown to his fellow passengers, he has been recruited by the CIA for foreign surveillance activities, and is now going back home with vital information concerning Russia's designs in the Far East. For national security reasons, his real identity has been revealed only to the Captain. Otherwise he would have remained an ordinary tourist on board ship.

LUIS ARIENTO ... age 22. Cuban refugee, unofficially regarded as the most promising baseball player in the American League. Like the late Clemente, he thrills millions with his pyrotechnics at bat, on the basepaths, and in the centerfield. He is completing a tour of the USA and the Philippines, urging youngsters to "turn off" drugs.

MIMSY STAR ... age 24. (Formerly Zosia Chmielinski from Chicago.) A sometime hooker and heroin addict (now reformed and rehabilitated) and currently "sex goddess" of film and stage. In a recent article in *Time* the following description was offered: "Her natural blend of earthy substantiality and childlike innocence makes her the first real successor to Marilyn Monroe as that unique kind of starlet that holds both male and female audiences in the palm of her hand.... in these times of economic depression and social oppression, Miss Starr has furnished millions with an escape from worldly cares..."

HAROLD GOODMAN ... age 21. Graduated from Yale at age of 20 with a B.A. and M.A. in political science. Current leader and social director of the Youth International Party. His M.A. thesis was entitled "The New Anarchy or Else." It has been acclaimed as a political landmark by the *New York Review of Books* and designated as "must reading" by *National Review*.

Discussion

Which five persons did you select? Why? How were your selections made? What characteristics of the twelve characters were particularly important? Why? How are they reflected in your final selections? In what ways were your decisions reflective of your values, stereotypes, and attitudes? What role did values play in your perceptions of the twelve characters? During group considerations what was the impact of values upon the discussion? What aspects of this exercise have relevance for everyday communication dynamics?

5. Meaning and Category Formation

This exercise is designed to provide a basis for discussions of the nature of meaning and the process by which categories are formed. The activity can be used with any number of participants and requires approximately 45 minutes.

Procedure

1. Basically, the exercise involves participants in discovering the meaning of "ZIF" which is a label for a category of geometric forms. The referrents for "ZIF" are determined by the instructor prior to the exercise, and by asking "yes" or "no" questions, and through a process of logical—and sometimes illogical—thinking, participants attempt to determine the definition.
2. Using the forms provided in Worksheet 5.1 as the basic ingredients, the instructor selects a particular configuration which appears in some of the forms, but not in others—and calls that ZIF. ZIF may be a vertical line with a left-branching appendage, for example.

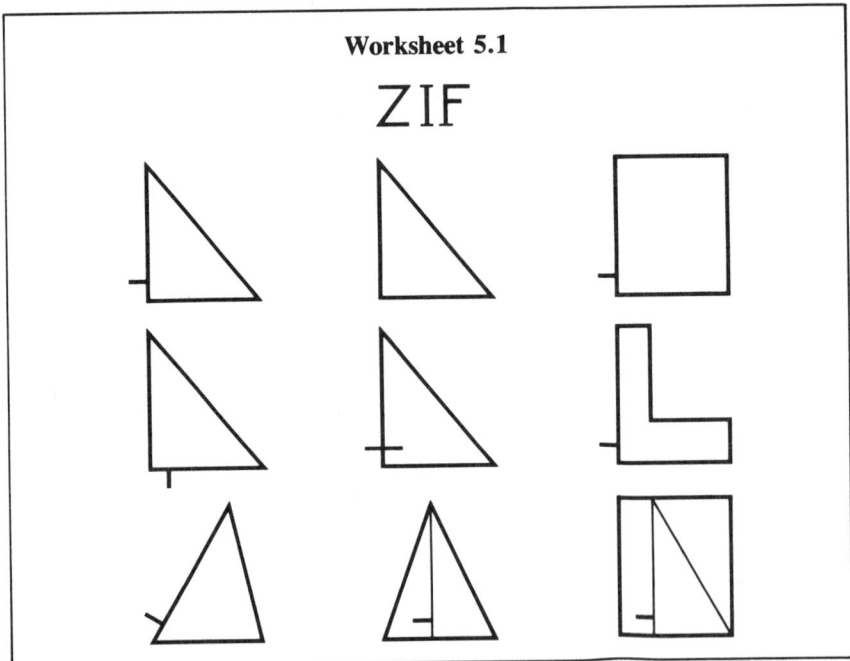

3. The instructor does not reveal the identity of ZIF, but distributes to each participant copies of the Worksheet or places the forms on a flip chart or blackboard.

4. Participants are told that their task is to discover the meaning of the term ZIF, and that they may gather information from the instructor—who knows what a ZIF is—by asking questions which can be answered with a "yes" or "no".
5. Proceed with question and answer session until ZIF is defined and the category understood, or as appropriate to the goals of the instructor.

Discussion

Was the meaning of ZIF discovered? How? Which shapes contain ZIFs? What process was followed to define which geometric configurations? How is meaning formed? What role does experience play in the formation of personal meanings? How do we check to confirm whether others share these meanings? Where do meanings and categories reside? In objects, words, etc.? In people? Can meanings be fully shared? How did the processes, which took place in this exercise, parallel those in everyday communication experiences?

The instructor may wish to repeat the exercise, following discussion, utilizing a different definition of ZIF—a 90° angle, for example—to illustrate the stability of categories once formed, and the difficulty of "unlearning."

6. Perceptual Patterning

The objective of this exercise is to increase participant awareness of the dynamics of intrapersonal communication. The exercise can be used with groups of 5 to 10 participants, and requires approximately 30 minutes to complete.

Procedure
1. The instructor or members of each group select several reasonably familiar objects which are small enough to be easily manageable with one or two hands.
2. One of the items is placed in the center of a seated group of participants, who are encouraged to pick up the object spontaneously, when they see a new or unusual way to look at or think about the object. Each indicates non-verbally, his or her concept of the object—a pair of scissors is portrayed as a pair of glasses or a ball of string is manipulated to appear as a yo-yo, for example—and the process continues from one person to another in the group until all possible concepts for an object seem to the group to be exhausted.
3. Another object becomes the group focus, then another, and so on.

Discussion

This activity can be viewed as a type of brainstorming of fantasy exercise where the familiar is reconceived in terms of the unfamiliar. A paper clip, a pair of scissors, a Christmas tree ornament, a piece of chalk, a cotterpin, or a "slinky" can be "understood" differently, only with some effort. Of course, the primary value of the exercise is to highlight for discussion the nature of perceptual patterning, the stability of those perceptual patterns, the difficulties of altering them, and the processes by which such changes may occur.

What difficulties were encountered? Why would it be difficult to perceive of or conceive of familiar objects in different ways? For what purposes might it be valuable to develop skills for doing so? Under what circumstances might there be demands for relearning of the familiar in everyday communication situations?

7. Language and Meaning

This exercise is intended to highlight for discussion the ambiguities of language and the manner in which people create the meanings they attach to words. Additionally, it provides the basis for noting the different meanings that different persons may attach to the same word. The activity can be used with any number of participants and requires approximately 20 minutes to complete.

Procedure

1. Distribute copies of the accompanying Worksheet 7.1 to participants, with instructions to read and individually answer each question as they believe to be appropriate. Allow five minutes for completion.
2. Compile and compare participant's responses on a blackboard or flip chart, and discuss.

Worksheet 7.1

LANGUAGE AND MEANING

Instructions:

Read and answer each question as best you can from your own point of view.

1. The student government president was elected by an overwhelming majority.
   What percentage of the vote did he receive?

2. John is a heavy marijuana user.
   How often does he smoke?

3. Mr. Johnson gives an unusually large number of exams in his course.
   How many exams does he give?

4. Mary has a well paying job.
   How much does she earn annually?

5. Dr. Wenden is middle-aged.
   How old is he?

6. Mary's grade-point-average is excellent.
   What is her average?

7. Jackson dropped out of school very early.
   How many years of school did he complete?

Discussion

Why were there different responses to the same question? What role did the *words* themselves play in this outline? What role did the individual's past experience play? How did participants decide upon the answers they selected? Do the answers one selects say anything about the individual giving the answers? What? Discuss. How does this basic process relate to everyday communication situations?

8. Message Set

This exercise is intended to highlight for discussion the nature of communicative behaviors that become habit, and to provide the basis for exploration of the origins and consequences of message response sets. The activity can be used with any number of participants and requires 15–30 minutes to complete.

Procedure

1. Distribute to each participant a copy of the "How to Follow Instructions" Worksheet (8.1), with instructions that they are to be kept face down on the desk, in front of each participant, and that no one is to look at the *exam* or begin until the instructor permits it.
2. When all participants have a worksheet face down before them, the instructor looks at his or her watch, and says "Everybody ready? Begin."
3. Allow five minutes or as needed for completion of the "Exam."

Worksheet 8.1

HOW TO FOLLOW INSTRUCTIONS

Instructions:

This test is designed to test your ability to think *accurately* and *carefully*. Since it is very probable that you have never taken *this type* of test before, failure to read the instructions CAREFULLY may lower your score.

1. You will read a brief story. Assume that all of the information presented in the story is definitely accurate and true. Read the story carefully. You may refer back to the story whenever you wish.
2. You will then read statements about the story. Answer them in numerical order. DO NOT GO BACK to fill in answers or to change answers.
3. After you read carefully each statement, determine whether the statement is:
    (a) True—meaning: On the basis of the *information presented in the story* the statement is DEFINITELY TRUE.
    (b) False—meaning: On the basis of the *information presented in the story* the statement is DEFINITELY FALSE.
    (c) Questionable—meaning: The statement MAY be true (or false) but on the basis of the *information presented in the story* you cannot be *definitely certain*. (If any part of the statement is doubtful, mark the statement "Questionable.")

Discussion

What happened? How many participants believe they passed the exam? How many participants wrote their name in the upper right hand corner? Why? Were there instructor-provided cues which contributed to the response pattern? What role did past experience play in bringing about the pattern of habit responses? Did participants notice the instructor glance at his or her watch? Did the gesture send a message to some? How do communication habits develop? Do they serve a useful purpose? Are they easily alterable? What are some advantages to being more aware of one's own communication habits? Are there any disadvantages?

It may be useful to couple this exercise with instructions to participants to be aware of and record some of their communication habits during the next day or so, noting especially those which seem most and least useful.

9. Observation and Inference

This activity is designed to focus on processes of observation and inference as they relate to intrapersonal communication. The activity can be used with any number of participants and requires approximately one hour to complete.

Procedure

1. Distribute copies of Worksheet 8.1, one to each participant.
2. Read over "Instructions" in handout aloud to be certain that all participants are clear as to the nature of the task.
3. Ask participants to complete the *Sample Test*. See Worksheet 9.1.
4. Ask participants to begin working through the *Test Story A*. Remind participants that the statements must be evaluated in numerical order, and that they may not change an evaluation once it has been made. They may, however, reread the story as often as they like. Allow 15 minutes for participants to complete the test.

Worksheet 9.1

THE TEST

Story (A)

A certain west coast university scientist chartered a ship for exploration purposes. When a large white bird was sighted the scientist asked permission to kill it. He stated that the white albatrosses are usually found only off the east coast of Australia. He wanted the bird as a specimen for the university museum.

The crew protested against the killing of the bird, calling the scientist's attention to the old sea superstition that bad luck followed the killing of a white albatross.

Nevertheless the captain granted permission to kill the bird and the bird was killed. These mishaps happened after the bird was killed:
    The net cables fouled up three times.
    The net caught on the bottom and was ripped to shreds.
    The shaft of the main winch snapped and it took the crew members five hours to reel in by hand 1,700 feet of cable.
    A rib was broken when Jackie Larson, a scientific aide, fell down a hatch ladder.
    The scientist became seasick for the first time in his life.
    Lost gear forced the ship to head for land.
    The cook left his job.

Statements About Story A

1. The scientist had never been seasick before.
2. The purpose of the voyage was primarily pleasure and sight-seeing.
3. The story lists various incidents which follow the killing of the bird.
4. After the scientist shot the albatross the troubles happened.
5. No scientist's name was mentioned in the story.
6. The scientist was surprised to see a white albatross in the vicinity.

7. The scientist asked the captain's permission to kill the bird.
8. The scientist was not from a university or a college.
9. It took the crew members less than five minutes to reel in the seventeen hundred feet of cable.
10. A lost gear made it necessary for the ship to return to the west coast.
11. Fortunately, the net cables never fouled up.
12. A ship was chartered by a scientist.
13. The net was ripped on the bottom of the sea.
14. The cook was fired because of his objection to the killing of the bird.
15. Larson broke a leg.
16. After the bird was killed the mishaps occurred.
17. The white albatross was sighted near Australia.
18. When an albatross was sighted flying near the ship the scientist asked permission to kill it.
19. The net was not damaged.
20. The troubles happened after the albatross was killed.
21. The scientist was less influenced by the old sea superstition than were the members of the crew.
22. The ship, propelled by a motor, was in difficulty after the gear broke.
23. Permission to kill the bird was given by the captain.
24. Seventeen hundred feet of cable were reeled in by hand.
25. The bird that was killed was an albatross.
26. The sailors were not disturbed when the scientist violated the old sea superstition.
27. The person who fell down a hatch ladder was a man named Larson.
28. Larson broke one of the ribs of the ship.
29. The scientist did not want the bird as a specimen for the university museum.
30. The naturalist did not charter the ship.
31. The scientist did not ask the crew for permission to kill the albatross.
32. The scientist's attention was called to the old sea superstition that bad luck follows the killing of a white albatross.
33. The naturalist did not ask permission to kill the bird in order to secure it as a museum specimen.
34. The scientist expected to see a white albatross in that vicinity.
35. The scientist was influenced by the warnings of the crew.
36. The cook did not leave his job.
37. The captain broke one of his ribs.
38. The bird was killed against the captain's orders.
39. The crew members were only trying to frighten the scientist by protesting against the killing of the bird.
40. A lost gear was not the reason the ship landed.

Discussion

The discussion following the exercise should deal with the "errors" made in the exercise, exploring the extent to which communication processes occurring in this activity are typical in communication situations in the "real world." What assumptions affected the manner in which participants evaluated the statements? What aspects of the story contributed to problems in evaluation and inference? What precautions can be taken to avoid making incorrect assumptions, observations, and inferences? Do our assumptions about other people influence the way we talk to and listen to them? What are the origins of such assumptions?

10. Listening I

This exercise is designed to demonstrate some of the problems involved with listening and word interpretation. It takes about 10 minutes and can be used with groups of any size.

Procedure

The instructor asks participants to:
1. "Write a small i and dot it."
2. Their task is to correctly follow the instructions.
3. After the group has completed the exercise, ask for correct solutions.

Discussion

When you write a small "i" you automatically dot it. So, the only way to fully follow the statement as read is to put a *second* dot above the "small i." One could also write "a small eye" and dot it. Why do these problems of listening and word interpretation occur? Is there one correct answer? How do we decide?

11. Listening II

This exercise is also designed to underscore some of the problems involved with listening and word interpretation. It takes about 10 minutes and can be used with groups of any size.

Procedure

1. The group is instructed to: "Draw a short vertical line to represent a mama bull, a papa bull, and a baby bull."
2. Their task is to correctly follow the instructions.
3. After the group has completed the exercise, ask for correct solutions.

Discussion

Anyone drawing three lines interprets a MAMA BULL as being possible. There are not any mama *bulls*. In addition, the lines may be of varied length—normally the mama bull is a medium-sized vertical line, the papa bull the longest, and the baby bull the shortest. Why? There is nothing in the statement to indicate size variation, yet preset concepts concerning "mama," "papa," and "baby" tend to lead to the length variation. Was the group also tempted to follow impossible instructions?

12. Listening III

This exercise is designed to indicate some of the problems involved with listening to complex information.

Procedure

1. The class is instructed to answer the following problem: "You are driving a bus. You go east 12 miles, you turn south and go 2 miles and take on 9 passengers, then you turn west and go 3 miles and let off 4 passengers. How old is the bus driver?"
2. After the class has completed the exercise, ask for solutions.

Discussion

Most listeners will attempt to follow the numbers and arrive at a solution based on them. The actual solution is the *age of each listener*. The problem uses the word "you" four times. What is the relationship between listening and interpretation? Why did people fail to hear the term "you?" What are the implications for any orally delivered instructions?

13. Listening IV

This exercise provides an opportunity to heighten participant sensitivities to the process and problems of listening. The activity can be used with any number of participants and requires about 45 minutes.

Procedure

1. Read the story in Worksheet 13.1 to the group, explaining first that it will be followed by a listening test.
2. Distribute the test form provided in Worksheet 13.2.
3. After participants complete the Worksheet, discuss the correct answers.
4. Discussion may accompany, or follow, presentation of correct responses.

Worksheet 13.1

LISTENING: THE TURNPIKE ARREST CASE

A man in a car stopped for speeding and the state trooper who flagged it down, were shot yesterday during a pistol duel alongside the New Jersey Turnpike in *Mount Laurel* (5). The wounded civilian and three companions escaped in *the policeman's patrol car* (3) but were captured and arrested shortly after they sped through a tollgate and left the superhighway.

The four face charges of assault with intent to kill.

Trooper Patrick Keane, 38, was shot *once* (7) in the *leg* (1) with a *.22-caliber pistol* (2). He was listed in good condition in *Garden State Community Hospital* (8) in Marlton.

Also listed in good condition at the same hospital was Rayfield Fenderburk, 24, of Charlotte, N.C., who was shot once in *the abdomen* (4).

State police Lt. Gordon Hector said the shooting in the Burlington County community occurred after Keane stopped a *1971 canary-yellow northbound car* (10) for speeding. When the auto stopped, the trooper spotted a chrome-plated pistol on the front seat and ordered the men out of the car, Hector said.

Keane, an eight-year veteran of the force, called for support and had handcuffed two of the men. The others began scuffling with the trooper, Hector said, and shooting began.

After Keane was wounded, the four men piled into the patrol car, Hector said, and sped through a tollbooth at the Mount Laurel exit.

The *toll taker* (9) alerted the state police who also had been told of the incident by a *passing motorist from Maryland* (9), Hector said.

The four men were captured by four Mount Laurel policemen after they drove into an industrial park near the turnpike.

Taken into custody along with Funderburk, were his brother Leon, 21, Larry Frazier, 24, of Manhattan, and Charles Taylor, 30, of Charlotte.

A chrome-plated .22 caliber pistol was found in the car with *cash* amounting to *$2,000* **(6)** and a quantity of drugs, police said.

Hector said they were investigating the possibility of the money being the proceeds of a robbery.

Keane lives near Moorestown and is married.

The four were arraigned before Cherry Hill Township Municipal Judge James Greenberg last night, with *bail* set at *$250,000* **(11)** each. They are all being *held at Camden County Jail* **(12)**, Camden, with the exception of Funderburk, who is still hospitalized in Marlton.

Worksheet 13.2

LISTENING TEST

1. The trooper was shot in what part of his body?_____
2. What kind of weapon was used to shoot the trooper?_____
3. The wounded suspect and three companions made their escape in what?_____
4. The suspect was shot in what part of his body?_____
5. At what location on the New Jersey Turnpike did this incident take place?_____
6. How much cash was found in the car?_____
7. How many times was the trooper shot?_____
8. In what hospital is the policeman being treated?_____
9. Two different people alerted the police about the shooting? They were: _____ and _____
10. What kind of car was stopped for speeding by the trooper?_____
11. How much bail was set for each suspect?_____
12. In what jail are the suspects being held?_____

Discussion

Was the exam difficult? Why? What were the major problems? Were some questions more often missed than others? What explanation might be advanced? What are some additional factors that contribute to listening errors?

PART 2

SOCIAL COMMUNICATION

If *personal communication* focuses upon the symbolic relationship between an individual and his or her environment, *social communication* centers on the symbolic activities of individuals with one another. To a large extent, the environment with which humans organize, and must deal, is the product of the social endeavors of other persons. This is as true for *architecture, automobiles,* and *technology* of all sorts, as it is for *words, meanings, norms, laws, customs,* and *ethics*. The creation of each requires joint action among two or more persons, and this is the domain of interpersonal or social communication.

Coordinated activity by two or more persons is the one element which characterizes any of the various social units which one may wish to better understand. Whether one speaks of a friendship, a dating relationship, a marital dyad, a small group, a family, an organization, a society, or an international system, all have in common that they exist only through the coordination of the activities of diverse individuals.

The development, maintenance, elaboration or deterioration of each of these relationships occurs through communication. Social communication is as central to the confused first impressions two strangers may have of one another when first they meet, as it is to the rather substantial degree of coordinated understandings that are possible if the relationship continues for many years. The nature of each dyad member's *dress, mannerisms, language, language-usage patterns, gestures, body positions, topics of conversation, eye-contact patterns*—and the meanings and significances each person attaches to them—are products of social communication. To a large extent, we do what we do because we have learned those behaviors through social interaction with other persons.

In this context, the socializing function of early social communication experiences with family, friends, and teachers, are critical forces in shaping an individual's knowledge, beliefs, attitudes, and values—his meanings for the people and things around him or her. While the outcomes of this process may be particularly dramatic in one's early years, these influences continue throughout life in educational, professional, political, and religious contexts.

Particularly in social relationships involving only a few or several persons, each individual involved has considerable power and responsibility for shaping the directions social systems take. In friendships, dating dyads, families, small groups, and organizations, the way one person behaves can significantly influence the other members of the social unit, and therefore, the relationship as a whole.

Presumably, the more conscious one is of the nature of social communication processes, the more able and capable one is to facilitate the creation or evolution of increasingly productive and satisfying social relationships. The activities included in this section of *Human Communication Handbook* are intended to serve this function as they provide an increased awareness of some dimensions of social communication and heightened understanding of the role they play in communication outcomes. Exercises, games, and simulations in this section focus on self concept and self-disclosure, nonverbal cues and interpersonal prediction, dyadic communication, the physical contexts of social communication, selective perception and debate, communication roles, organizational roles and dynamics, leadership, decision-making, culture, values, and societal communication.

Bibliography

Berger, Peter L. and Thomas Luckmann, *The Social Construction of Reality,* Garden City: Doubleday, 1966.

Blumer, Herbert, *Symbolic Interactionism,* Englewood Cliffs: Prentice-Hall, 1969.

Blumer, Herbert, "Symbolic Interaction: An Approach to Human Communication," in *Approaches to Human Communication,* R. W. Budd and B. D. Ruben (Eds.), Rochelle Park, N.J.: Spartan/Hayden, 1972.

Duncan, Hugh D., *Symbols in Society,* London: Oxford University Press, 1968.

Goffman, Erving, *Relations in Public,* New York: Basic Books, 1971.

Ruben, Brent D., "Intrapersonal, Interpersonal, and Mass Communication Processes, in Individual and Multi-Individual Systems," in *General Systems Theory and Human Communication,* B. D. Ruben and J. Y. Kim (Eds.), Rochelle Park, N.J.: Hayden, 1975.

Watzlawick, Paul, Janet Beavin, and Don D. Jackson, *Pragmatics of Human Communication,* New York: Norton, 1967.

14. Self-Concept and Self-Disclosure

This activity highlights aspects of the process of self-definition and provides a structured context in which self-disclosure and interpersonal interaction occur. Any number of individuals may participate. The exercise requires approximately 60 minutes to complete.

Procedure

1. Distribute copies of the Individual Coat-of-Arms Worksheet. (14.1)
2. Participants are asked to complete the answers to the seven questions given at the bottom of the worksheet, entering their responses in the appropriate section of their *Coat-of-Arms*. Participants are also asked not to write their names on their worksheets.

Worksheet 14.1

INDIVIDUAL COAT-OF-ARMS

[Shield divided into 7 numbered sections]

Instructions:

a. In section 1, list two things you do very well.
b. In section 2, list the one place you most enjoy being.
c. In section 3, list what you consider to be your greatest achievement in life.
d. In section 4, list the three individuals who have influenced you most.
e. In section 5, list the three things about you that you believe to be most important.
f. In section 6, list the two major goals you have for the next two years.
g. In section 7, list three words to describe how you see yourself in ten years.

3. Groups of 4 or 5 participants each are formed, and the Coats-of-Arms for each 4–5 person group redistributed within the cluster such that no individual receives his or her own.
4. In turn, each group member reads the information on the Coat-of-Arms he or she received, and tries to determine to whom the Coat-of-Arms belongs.
5. After each such attempt to guess the identity of the owner of a Coat-of-Arms, the group may wish to discuss the basis upon which guesses were made, and the information used by the guesser in arriving at his or her decision. When the correct individual is identified, further discussion may focus on the seven answers on the Coat-of-Arms as completed by the individual.
6. After each member of each group has read the Coat-of-Arms information, and attempted to match it to its author, summary discussion may be appropriate either in small groups or in a large grouping of all participants.

Discussion

Were the seven questions difficult to answer? Which were easiest? Which most difficult? How accurate were attempts to match information on Coats-of-Arms with the authors? How accurate were the guesses? On what basis were guesses made? Did stereotyping occur? How well did your Coat-of-Arms, taken as a whole, represent how you view yourself? Were some individuals more guarded with the sorts of information they provided on their Coat-of-Arms than others? What other aspects of one's self-concept could have been included in the Coats-of-Arms that would have increased its adequacy as a means of saying "Who you are?" How do the processes that operated during the exercise and discussion relate to aspects of everyday communication experiences?

15. Dyadic Communication

This exercise provides a structured context in which the normal processes of interpersonal interaction and self-disclosure occur in an accelerated fashion. The activity can also be used as the basis for discussions of the role of intrapersonal processes in dyadic communication. The exercise can be used with any number of pairs of participants and requires approximately 45 minutes for completion.

Procedure
1. Distribute copies of the accompanying Worksheet 15.1 to each participant.
2. Group participants in dyads and explain that they are to work through the tion, then the other person responds to the same question, until the pair has answered all questions.
3. After completing quesitons 1-18, each dyad is instructed to discuss the questions listed in the Discussion Section.

Worksheet 15.1

DYADIC COMMUNICATION

Instructions:

Alternatively answer each question or complete the statement.
1. If I walked into a book store and purchased a book for leisure reading the title would probably be...
2. If I stopped on the way to class to listen to a "soap box" speaker, the topic of his or her speech might well be...
3. Reading the evening paper I notice one article which particularly angers me. The article is probably about...
4. My favorite humorous television show is... because...
5. Of the serious programs, I prefer...
6. The last movie I really enjoyed was...
7. Probably my favorite film of all time is...
8. The last time I attended a party was... I found the party... because...
9. When I listen to the radio it is generally because...
10. Of the various groups I belong to, the one which gives me the most personal satisfaction is... because?
11. People who know me best think I'm...
12. At a party, my behavior can best be characterized as...
13. I would say my major communication strength is...
14. Being with people socially makes me feel...
15. Working with other people on a project leads me to feel...
16. When I work with other people I generally...
17. People who know me best think my greatest weakness is...
18. Probably the one thing I'd like most to change about my communicative behavior is...

Discussion

What three adjectives would best describe your dyad partner, based upon what you have learned about him or her during this exercise? How does this exercise compare to dyadic communication which occurs in your everyday experience? What insights from this exercise can contribute to the development of a relationship with your dyad partner? What learnings from this exercise can be applied in your interpersonal relationships in general?

16. Non-Verbal Cues and Stereotyping

This activity is designed to highlight for discussion the importance of non-verbal cues in intrapersonal information processing, and in communication in general. The activity can be used best with groups of 20–30 participants and requires approximately 30 minutes to complete.

Procedure

1. Distribute a copy of Worksheet 16.1 to each participant.
2. Select one or both of the photographs provided in Fig. 16.1 and Fig. 16.2 (or their equivalent) and display them one at a time before participants.
3. Participants are asked to carefully study each photograph and to list on their worksheets each non-verbal cue they note in the picture. In Fig. 16.1, for example, the doll, wet hair, Mickey Mouse emblem, and dark backdrop are among the more obvious non-verbal data points.

Worksheet 16.1

NON-VERBAL CUES AND INTERPERSONAL PREDICTION

Non-Verbal Cues	Information and Predictive Value
Fig _____	_____
Fig _____	_____
Fig _____	_____

Fig. 16.1

Fig. 16.2

Social Communication 79

4. Following each listed cue, participants are asked to indicate, on the worksheet what they think the cues says about the person in the picture, of what information value the cue is to an observer. For each cue they are also asked to indicate what predictions they might tentatively offer about the person pictured.
5. Additionally, participants may be asked to indicate three possible verbal questions or statements they might make to the person pictured if they were to encounter the person in real life. These questions or statements should make use of the information value of the non-verbal cues.
6. Additional photographs are displayed, and steps 3, 4, 5 repeated for each.

Discussion

How many different non-verbal cues were listed for Fig. 16.1? For Fig. 16.2? What were they? It may be useful to list them on a flip chart or blackboard. Of what information value was each? Here it will be useful to discuss the range of possible interpretations of a particular cue, and discuss the tentativeness of the informational predictions. Of what predictive value are these cues? How valid are predictions based upon them? To what extent do the predictions reflect the predictor's own past experience? His or her own cultural background? What other factors are reflected in these observations and predictions? How important are non-verbal cues to interpersonal communication? How many of the predictions we make about other people are based primarily on non-verbal cues? How useful is non-verbal data in everyday interpersonal communication? To what extent can non-verbal cues be manipulated by the sender? What aspects of this exercise have particular relevance to everyday communication situations?

17. Environment

This exercise is designed to highlight for discussion the intrapersonal communication processes involved in gathering information about one's physical environment. It can be used with up to 50 participants depending upon facilities, and requires approximately 30 minutes to complete.

Procedure

1. Participants are gathered in a large room. They are instructed to walk around without talking, and to gather as much data as they can about the environment and the people in it, using all of their perceptual senses. Allow approximately 5 minutes for data gathering.
2. Group participants in clusters of 5–10 persons each. Groups may be formed in a traditional means, as with counting off by numbers, or by some non-verbal component such as eye color, height, color of clothes, position in the room, etc., to highlight the goals of the exercise.
3. Each group is asked to select a secretary. The instructor provides pencil and paper to each participant.
4. Groups are asked to compile a list of as many of the things they observed, smelled, heard, and touched as they can in a five-minute period. It may be useful to caution participants that they are not to be concerned with whether they liked or disliked what they noted, but simply to describe the information sources.
5. After the five-minute period, secretaries are asked to read their lists to the larger group for purposes of comparison.

Discussion

Information can be transmitted by eyes, gestures, movement, sounds, colors, mannerisms, clothes, smells, room size and shape, etc. Often in normal situations we are oblivious to the influences of a wide range of non-verbal cues which we may encounter. What information sources did participants note most frequently? Were some senses more frequent information sources than others? Were more cues noted that pertain to the physical environment (the room and physical aspects) or the human environment (the people in the room)? What unusual observations were made? Why might certain cues have been noted more often than others? What cues were noted that relate to the gestures of participants in the room? What cues were noted that relate to facial displays? What cues were noted that related positionings of persons within the room? What cues relate to the things worn by persons? What were percentages of each of the above? Might the sorts of cues noted vary from one culture to the next? Why? Might the cues noted vary from one person to the next? Why? Can one infer anything about a person based upon the cues that the person notes in the environment? What are the relevancies of this exercise to the usual communication experiences which are encountered in daily interactions?

18. Roles

This exercise focuses upon the concept of roles and the communication dynamic through which roles are established, defined, and maintained. Additionally, the activity is useful for identifying the sources of expectation regarding an individual's role or roles, and for underscoring the nature of conflicting demands present in any situation. The exercise can be used with any number of participants, and requires approximately 45 minutes to complete.

Procedure

1. Identify a particular *role* to be explored with participants, for example, the student role, the son or daughter role, the work role, the parent role, etc. While it is not necessary for all participants to consider the same role, it is useful for several individuals, at least, to focus on identical roles to facilitate discussion.
2. Distribute copies of Worksheet 18.1.

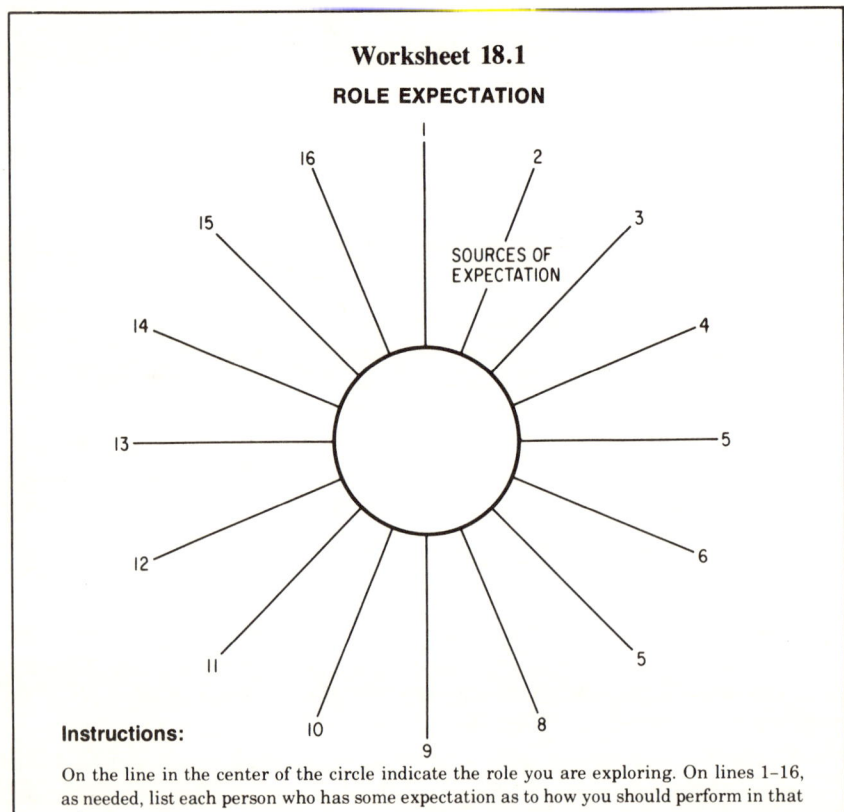

Worksheet 18.1

ROLE EXPECTATION

SOURCES OF EXPECTATION

Instructions:
On the line in the center of the circle indicate the role you are exploring. On lines 1-16, as needed, list each person who has some expectation as to how you should perform in that role.

3. Participants are asked to list on the radius lines of the Role Expectation Worksheet (18.1) each of those persons or institutions who in some fashion have ideas or expectations about the role being explored. The instructor may wish to give several examples: "If you're exploring your role as student, then you would list on the radius lines all those persons or institutions who have expectations as to how you should behave as a student. You might want to list each parent, each teacher, friends, etc."
4. After participants have individually completed the worksheet 18.1, distribute worksheet 18.2 on which participants list the *sources of expectation* identified on the previous worksheet and a brief summary of what each of the listed individual's expectations are.
5. Participants are grouped with others who have considered the same role. Where many or all participants are examining a single role, divide participants into discussion groups of approximately 3–6 persons each.

Worksheet 18.2

SPECIFIC EXPECTATIONS

Sources   *Expectation*

1. _____   _____
2. _____   _____
3. _____   _____
4. _____   _____
5. _____   _____
6. _____   _____
7. _____   _____
8. _____   _____
9. _____   _____
10. _____ _____
11. _____ _____
12. _____ _____
13. _____ _____
14. _____ _____
15. _____ _____
16. _____ _____

Instructions:

List the sources on lines 1–16 that were identified on the Role Expectation Worksheet. On the line following, summarize briefly the nature of the expectation each has for your behavior in the role under consideration.

6. Provide approximately 15 minutes for group members to compare their lists of sources and the expectations believed to be characteristic of each. Depending upon the goals of the instructor and the similarity or diversity of roles being explored, it may be useful to ask one individual from each group to summarize their group's discussion to other groups. This will be particularly useful when the roles under study are differing, yet perhaps interdependent, as with husband and wife, male and female, employer and employee, student and teacher, etc.

Discussion

How many sources of expectation were listed by individuals? By groups? Were there many differences between individual lists within groups? Between groups? What sources of expectation were listed? What expectations were attributed to each? By individuals? By groups? How much similarity is there between groups? Are there potential conflicts between various expectations? What are the possible or probable consequences of the conflicts for the sources? For the person who is the object of the expectations?

Where similar roles are under examination, it will be productive to explore the similarities and differences between the sources of role expectations for each. Who are the sources of expectation? How are the expectations similar? How do they differ? Are there conflicting expectations? What will be the probable consequences of these conflicts? For the individuals who are the objects of the expectations? For the sources of those expectations? How can these conflicting expectations be dealt with? What are the applications of specific material in this exercise to everyday communication situations? How can the results of the activity be applied?

19. Selective Perception, Debate, and Decision-Making

This exercise focuses upon the processes of gathering, perceiving, and interpreting information in formal decision-making. The exercise consists of two phases: (1) The initial assignment and team research; (2) Group consensus and a symposium debate. It can be used with any number of two to four person teams, but requires approximately one week between the initial assignment and the performance. Allow approximately two hours for phase 2.

Procedure

1. *Assignment:* Each two- to four-persons team is assigned to prepare a debate case on one side (either the negative or the affirmative) of the following resolution:
   Resolved: **Candidates for national political office should be required to hold public debates on the issues.**
   (At this time, the instructor or facilitator, depending upon his or her goals for the exercise, may elect to provide the group with an explanation of formal debate procedures and case preparation.)
2. *Team Research:* Each team is assigned to research the topic and to compile: (1) a definition of the terms of the resolution; (2) a minimum of five evidence cards; and (3) a file of their strongest arguments.
3. *Group Consensus:* As soon as the teams have completed their research (one week should be sufficient), they are brought together and formed into two groups: All the negative teams in one group and all the affirmative teams in another.
4. Each group will pool their resources (definitions, evidence, and arguments) in order to construct, through consensus, the "best" possible case. Allow approximately one hour for this process.
5. At the end of the allotted time, each group will select two spokespersons to present their case.
6. *Symposium Debate:* The spokespersons will engage in a debate on the assigned resolution. The facilitator or instructor may either serve as the moderator in this phase of the exercise or he or she may wish to appoint one of the participants to serve. The format is as follows:
   1. Introduction: the moderator introduces the resolution and the speakers.
   2. Opening Statements: a spokesperson from the affirmative team and then a spokesperson from the negative team make 6–8 minute presentations of their cases.
7. *Cross Examination:* Each side is given 10 minutes to question the other; affirmative begins the questioning.
8. *Summary Statements:* Each side summarizes their position; negative speaks first.

9. *Audience Forum:* Audience is given 10–15 minutes to question the spokespersons.
10. *Closing Statement:* The moderator summarizes the issues and positions of the two teams (approximately 5 minutes).
11. *Evaluation:* The audience is asked to complete the following questions: Which side won the debate? Which side had the stronger arguments? Which side had the best evidence? Which side do you believe in? Which side did you believe in before you began your research? Which side did you research?

Discussion

The questionnaire should be sufficient stimulus to begin the discussion. However, it may be necessary to guide the discussion away from the contest of the debate resolution, toward the interpretation of the results.

Studies reveal that prior exposure to information, especially to information slanted toward one side of an issue, generally tends to bias the receiver in his or her interpretation of subsequent information. Further, constructing a message on one side of an issue, for a minimal reward, tends to lead to greater attitude change and/or higher levels of adherence. Did most people perceive that "their" side won? Did most people "believe in" the side that they researched? Did anyone "change their mind" as a result of the debate? Why? Why not? (It is useful to ask a volunteer to tabulate the results of the questionnaire at this point.)

Every way of seeing is also a way of not seeing; looking for information on one side of an issue tends to bias the researcher in his interpretation of whatever information he finds. Communities, whether based on living patterns, or on age, occupation, socio-economic levels, etc., tend to expose themselves to similar kinds and sources of information. In the cross-examination and audience forum stages, was any "new" information revealed? In the consensus exercise, were people willing to share information? Was it difficult to agree on the "best" evidence? "Best" arguments? How were the spokespersons chosen? Did they accurately represent their respective groups? Did teams seem to have searched out the same evidence? What sources were most commonly used? Did the teams search out contradictory evidence? That is, did the affirmatives look for and study negative evidence?

Given the results of the exercise, it is possible to conclude that "logical" proof (evidence) is as subject to selective interpretation as is "emotional" or "ethical" proof. Does the group now feel differently, or the same, about the relative merits of the resolution? In what ways is debate a useful method of decision-making? In what ways is it not useful?

20. Organizational Roles and Perceptions of Leadership and Followership

This exercise is intended to facilitate the exploration of the interrelationship between leader and follower roles in a group, team, or organizational context. Additionally, the activity may be used to explore particular dynamics of an ongoing group or unit. The exercise requires approximately one hour and is used to greatest advantage of intact groups or organizational units.

Procedure

1. Copies of the Perceptions of Leadership Worksheet (20.1) are distributed to participants. Five minutes are provided for completing the form.

Worksheet 20.1

ORGANIZATIONAL ROLES: PERCEPTIONS OF LEADERSHIP

Instructions:

For each statement, indicate whether you strongly agree (5), agree somewhat (4), are neutral (3), disagree somewhat (2), or strongly disagree (1).

- _____The leader should transmit his or her knowledge and know-how to those over whom he or she has authority or rank.
- _____It is impossible to define the leadership role out of context. Only with a specific knowledge of the situation can one specify the nature of good leadership.
- _____The leader should involve himself socially with work groups and strive to become perceived as "one of the guys" by those over whom he or she has responsibility.
- _____Primarily, the task of the leader is to model appropriate behavior.
- _____First and foremost, the leader is an agent of change.
- _____The leader must inspire motivation and competence in those over whom he or she has responsibility.
- _____The leader should strive to be replaceable by those over whom he or she has responsibility.
- _____The leader's only function is to coordinate those over whom he or she has responsibility, in order to get the job done.
- _____Essentially the leader should be at the service of those over whom he or she has responsibility, and should strive to insure that their work-related needs are being fulfilled.
- _____The leader should strive to actively involve those over whom he or she has responsibility in major decision-making.

---

2. Participants are grouped in small discussion groups in one of several ways, based upon the purposes of the exercise. If the activity is used mainly to facilitate a theoretical discussion of the interrelationship of leadership and followership, groupings can be made simply on the basis of convenience with 5–7 participants per group. Where the goal is to explore ongoing

leadership-followership dynamics of a particular unit, discussion groups should be composed of all members of the unit, including the leader. Where several units are involved, a similar option may be followed. Alternatively, in such circumstances, one or two discussion groups can be composed only of leaders, and the other discussion groups may then be made up of individuals over whom the leaders have responsibility.
3. Members of discussion groups are encouraged to compare their responses to items on the worksheet 20.1 and explore one another's reasoning. Depending upon group size, approximately 15 minutes should be adequate for discussion.
4. Where discussion groups are composed of intact groups or units, stress should be placed on the importance of exploring differences between the perceptions of the leader and those of the other members of the team.

Worksheet 20.2

ORGANIZATIONAL ROLES: PERCEPTIONS OF GROUP MEMBERSHIP

Instructions:

For each statement indicate whether you strongly agree (5), agree somewhat (4), are neutral (3), disagree somewhat (2), or strongly disagree (1).

_____ The team member should always be receptive to the group leader's instructions, suggestions, and know-how.

_____ Appropriate behavior for team members depends upon the kind of leadership present, and cannot be specified in any general way without knowing precisely what patterns of leadership will be operating in a given situation.

_____ Team or group members should strive to model their own behavior after that of the leader.

_____ Changes should generally be initiated by group or team members rather than by the leader or manager.

_____ Group members themselves have the primary responsibility for their own motivation, and the continued acquisition of information they need to perform capably in their positions.

_____ Members of the work group should expect to be provided with strong, continuing, leadership.

_____ The only important responsibility of a work group member is to get their own jobs done.

_____ The work group member should strive to facilitate the leader's needs and goals being met.

_____ Team members should actively strive to involve the leader in social and informal activities and treat him or her as "one of the guys."

_____ Members of the work group should actively strive to acquire a level of skill and knowledge equal to that of the leader with the goal of being able to replace him or her.

5. As discussions wind-down, the instructor may request the group to develop a brief summary of their discussions, highlighting differences and similarities between perceptions of the leader and other team members.
6. Where more than one discussion group is involved, ask one individual from each group to present a summary of their discussions to the other groups.
7. Distribute copies of the Group Member Worksheet 20.2 and repeat steps 1 through 6.

Discussion

Discussion may focus either upon theoretical or pragmatic issues related to the relationship between leadership and followership. To what extent do group members agree on what constitutes appropriate member behavior? How do these perceptions match the perceptions of the leader as to what is appropriate team member behavior? Do group members share in common a perception of the role of the leader? How well do these match the perceptions of the leader?

If the activity is used with intact groups, it is important to focus attention on those areas where most team members share a perception which is different from that of their leader. These are potential problem areas. Those topics where team members agree in their perception, and that perception is held also by the leader, are areas of commonness and may be explored as means of lessening barriers in the areas of difference.

21. Sex Role Perceptions

This exercise is intended to facilitate the exploration of the interrelationship between male and female sex roles. Additionally, the activity may be used to explore particular dynamics of an ongoing relationship. The exercise requires approximately one hour and is used to greatest advantage in intact groups or organizational units.

Procedure

1. Distribute copies of the Sex Roles Female Worksheet (21.1) to participants. Five minutes are provided for completing the form.
2. Participants are grouped in small discussion groups in one of several ways, based upon the purposes of the exercise. If the activity is used mainly to facilitate a theoretical discussion of the female role in society, groupings can be made simply on the basis of convenience with 5–7 participants per group. Where the goal is to explore ongoing male–female dynamics of a particular relationship, discussion groups should be dyads with both members of each relationship. Where several couples are involved, a similar option may be followed. Alternatively, in such circumstances, one or two discussion groups can be composed only of females and the other discussion groups may then be made up of males.

Worksheet 21.1

SEX ROLE PERCEPTIONS: THE FEMALE

Instructions:

For each statement indicate whether you strongly agree (5), agree somewhat (4), are neutral (3), disagree somewhat (2), or strongly disagree (1).

_____A primary role of the female ought to be to provide meaningful support for the males in her life—father, friends, husband and family.

_____A woman's major role should be to contribute equally to the solution of all problems encountered by her male friends, spouse, and/or family.

_____The female's only reeponsibility should be to provide for her own financial and psychological well-being, leaving the males or other females in her life to handle their responsibilities for themselves.

_____Pursuing personal growth and self-development should be the major component in the female's role.

_____To be effective, the female should strive to be flexible and function consistently with the definitions of her role that are thought to be appropriate by society and the persons with whom she comes into contact.

_____The female should devote herself to activities which have as the primary goal the facilitation of increased awareness and personal growth of other women.

3. Members of discussion groups are encouraged to compare their responses to items on the Worksheet and explore one another's reasoning. Depending upon group size, approximately 15 minutes should be adequate for discussion.
4. Where discussion groups are composed of intact groups or units, stress should be placed on the importance of exploring differences between the perceptions of the leader and those of the other members of the team.
5. As discussions wind-down, the instructor may request the group to develop a brief summary of their discussions, highlighting differences and similarities between perceptions of males and females.
6. Where more than one discussion group is involved, ask one individual from each group to present a summary to the other groups.
7. Distribute copies of the Sex Roles: Males Worksheet 21.2 and repeat steps 1 through 6.

Worksheet 21.2

SEX ROLE PERCEPTIONS: THE MALE

Instructions:

For each statement indicate whether you strongly agree (5), agree somewhat (4), are neutral (3), disagree somewhat (2), or strongly disagree (1).

_____ Pursuing one's own personal and professional advancement and development should be the major life activity of the male.
_____ The male should devote a majority of his life ensuring that the females in his life—friends, mother, wife etc.—do not want for lack of money, housing and clothing.
_____ The male should be willing to share equally all decisions with females in his life.
_____ To be successful the male should tailor his mode of operating to the demands society and others he encounters place upon him.
_____ The male should endeavor to facilitate, as much as possible, the increased awareness and personal growth of other men.
_____ The male role should consist centrally of the pursuit of personally-defined happiness and pleasure.

Discussion

Discussion may focus either upon theoretical or pragmatic issues related to the female–male relationship and problems of sex roles. To what extent do males agree on what constitutes appropriate male roles? How do these perceptions match the perceptions of females as to what is an appropriate male role? Do females share in common a perception of the role of the male? How well do these match the perceptions of males?

If the activity is used with couples, it is important to focus attention on those areas where they differ in perceptions. These are potential problem areas. Those topics where they share a common perception of sex roles may be explored as means of lessening barriers in the areas of perceptual difference.

22. Values, Vocational Roles and Group Decision-Making

This exercise is designed to provide a context in which to explore the dynamics of individual and group decision-making. The activity requires approximately 45 minutes and can be used with groups of 5 to 10 persons. Each group should be seated in a circle or around a table.

Procedure

1. Distribute Worksheet 22.1 one per participant. Participants are grouped in clusters of from 5 to 10 persons.
2. Each group is asked to read and carefully consider the "Right to Strike" scenario provided on Worksheet 22.1. Remind participants to rank the 15 vocational roles in order, from the role for whom strikes are most justified (1), through the vocation where strikes are least appropriate (15).
3. After all groups have completed their rankings, a representative from each group reports their rankings and rationale to members of other groups.

Worksheet 22.1

RIGHT TO STRIKE

You are the labor committee of the House of Representatives. A bill to clarify the right to strike for different occupational roles has been introduced and your committee has been asked for its recommendation. This is an election year and you must carefully weigh your decision as each decision (choice) will have to be justified. Rank the following occupational groups according to the group with the most right to strike through the group with the least right to strike. (1-15)

_____ 1. Firemen   _____ 9. Teachers

_____ 2. Oil field workers   _____ 10. Garbage men

_____ 3. Farm labor   _____ 11. Truck drivers

_____ 8. Doctors   _____ 12. Construction workers

_____ 4. Aircraft industry workers _____ 13. State employees

_____ 5. Retail sales clerks   _____ 14. Gas station owners

_____ 6. Bus drivers   _____ 15. Barbers

_____ 7. Policemen

Discussion

This exercise is a stimulant for discussions of various vocational roles, and the value participants attach to the appropriateness of the right to strike for each. The activity also provides an excellent opportunity to focus on decision-making. What methods did the group use in its attempts at decision-making? Which methods were most effective? How accurately does the final ranking reflect the input of the group members? Were some group members more influential than others? What sorts of leadership patterns emerged? How did the group tolerate views which may have differed from the majority? How comfortable are group members with the final ranking? Were these actually to be recommendations to the Congress? Why? What are the implications of this? How does this activity relate to everyday communication situations? What role do values and personal involvement play in individual and group decision-making?

23. Organizational Decision-making

This exercise is designed to provide participants an opportunity to focus upon the dynamics of decision-making within an organizational context where resources are scarce and power unevenly distributed. The game requires approximately 50 minutes and may be used with any number of participants.

Procedure

1. Distribute a copy of Worksheet 23.1 to each participant, with verbal instructions to read carefully the description of the game situation and the roles which will be involved. Allow 5–10 minutes for participants to familiarize themselves with the problem.
2. Place participants in groups of six persons each.
3. For each group, appoint one person to take the role of the *foreman*.
4. Instruct the *foreman* that he or she is to select persons to play each of the other roles; *George, Bill, John, Mary, Hank*.
5. Inform the participant groups that they have thirty minutes for discussion, at the end of which the foreman will announce his or her decision.
6. Depending upon the instructor's goals and the number of participants, it may be useful to ask the foreman from each group to report their decision to the other groups along with their rationale, prior to a general discussion.

Worksheet 23.1

ORGANIZATIONAL DECISION-MAKING: THE NEW TRUCK DILEMMA

You work for the telephone company and one of you will be the foreman while the others will be repairmen. The job of a repairman is to fix phones that are out of order. The job requires knowledge and diagnostic skills as well as muscular skills. Repairmen must climb telephone poles, work with small tools, and meet customers. The foreman of a crew is usually an ex-repairman and this happens to be true in this case. He has an office at the garage location but spends a good deal of time making the rounds, visiting the places where the men are working. Each repairman works alone and ordinarily does several jobs in a day. The foreman gives the help and instructions needed.

The repairmen drive to the various locations in the city to do repair work. Each of them drives a small truck and takes pride in keeping it looking good. The repairmen have a possessive feeling about their trucks and like to keep them in good running order. Naturally, the men like to have new trucks, because a new truck gives them a feeling of pride.

Here are some facts about the trucks and the crewmen that report to Walt Marshall, the supervisor of repairs:

George	17 years with the co., has a 2 year-old Ford truck
Bill	11 years with the co., has a 5 year-old Dodge truck
John	10 years with the co., has a 4 year-old Ford truck
Mary	5 years with the co., has a 3 year-old Ford truck
Hank	3 years with the co., has a 5 year-old Chevrolet truck

Most of them do all of their driving in the city, but John and Mary cover the jobs in the suburbs.

In acting your part in the role playing, accept the facts as given, as well as assuming the attitude supplied in your specific role. From this point on, let your feelings develop in accordance with the events that transpire in the role playing process. When facts or events arise that are not covered by the roles, make up things which are consistent with the way it might be in a real life situation.

WALT MARSHALL (Foreman)
You are the foreman of a crew of repairmen each of whom drives a small service truck to and from his various jobs. Every so often you get a new truck to exchange for an old one, and you have the problem of deciding to which of your crew you should give the new truck. Often there are hard feelings because each one seems to feel he is entitled to a new truck, so you have a tough time being fair. As a matter of fact, it usually turns out that whatever you decide, most of them consider it wrong. You now have to face the issue again because a new truck has just been allocated to you for distribution. The new truck is a Chevrolet.

In order to handle this problem, you have decided to put the decision to the crew themselves. You will tell them about the new truck and will put the problem in terms of what would be the fairest way to allocate the truck. Don't take a position yourself because you want to do what the crew thinks is the fairest.

GEORGE
When a new Chevrolet truck becomes available you think you should get it because you have most seniority and don't like your present truck. Your own car is a Chevrolet, and you prefer a Chevrolet truck such as you drove before you got the Ford.

BILL
You feel you deserve a new truck and it certainly is your turn. Your present truck is old, and since the more senior man has a fairly new truck, you should get the next one. You have taken excellent care of your present Dodge, and have kept it looking like new. A man deserves to be rewarded if he treats a company truck like his own.

JOHN
You have more driving to do than most of the other men because your work is in the suburbs. You have a fairly old truck and you feel you should have the new one because you do so much driving.

MARY
The heater in your present truck is inadequate. Since Hank backed into the door of your truck it has never been repaired to fit right. The door lets in too much cold air, and you attribute your frequent colds to this. You want to have a warm truck since you have a good deal of driving to do. As long as it has good tires, brakes, and is comfortable you don't care about the make.

HANK
You have the poorest truck in the crew. It is 5 years old, and before you got it, it had been in a bad wreck. It has never been good, and you've put up with it for three years. It's about time you got a good truck to drive, and it seems only fair that the next one should be yours. You have a good accident record. The only accident you had was when you sprung the door of Mary's truck when she opened it as you backed out of the garage. You hope the new truck is a Ford because you prefer to drive one.

Discussion

What decision did the foremen reach? What assumptions did that decision reflect? What values were stressed? What priorities underlined? How satisfied are the drivers with the decision? Are all equally satisfied? Why? Why not? Did coalitions arise, such as foremen vs. repairmen, senior drivers vs. younger drivers, etc.? What role did power and authority play in the outcome? What role did power and authority play in the interaction that occurred during the thirty-minute discussion period? How effectively did the foremen operate? How could their functioning have been improved? What strategies did the drivers utilize? How effective were they? Were there other strategies which might have been more effective? What were they? Here comparisons between the dynamics in different groups will prove useful. What aspects of this decision-making game apply to everyday communication situations? How typical is the basic situation described—one decision-maker with power, and several other individuals each of whom depend upon the leader for an opportunity to acquire scarce resources?

24. Organizational Dynamics

The self-instructional guide to organizational diagnosis is a structured information gathering inventory designed to highlight important dimensions of formal enterprises. The profile can be completed individually or through group activity.

Procedure

1. Distribute copies of the self-instructional guide to organizational diagnosis (Worksheet 24.1).
2. Participants complete profiles either individually or in groups.

Worksheet 24.1

ORGANIZATIONAL GUIDE

I. Formal Structure of Organization

1. What is the nature of the organizational chart?
2. What positions are listed?
3. Who presently occupies each?
4. What is the formal chain of command?
5. What is the scope of responsibility for each member of the organization?
6. To whom are you directly responsible?
7. Who is directly responsible to you?
8. Who are your counterparts?
9. Describe the flow of information within the organization. (How are decisions communicated?)
10. What formal mechanisms are utilized for achieving upward communication?
11. What are the various constituencies—organizational units, agencies, persons, interests, etc.—external to the organization which formally influence or are influenced by the organization?
12. What individuals within the organization are responsible for liaison with these constituencies?
13. Of these constituencies, which directly affect your activities within the organization?
14. Who has authority over these interfaces?

II. Informal Structure of Organization

1. Which positions within the organization are generally perceived as prestigious?
2. Which positions within the organization are generally perceived as lacking prestige?
3. Which individuals in the organization have high status?
4. Which individuals in the organization have low status?
5. What is the apparent basis for distinctions in 1-4?
6. What informal communication channels are operative (tennis, cocktail parties, rumor mill, coffee breaks, lunch chatter, etc.)?
7. How active are these channels?
8. What functions are fulfilled by these interactions?
9. How well does the content of informal channels correspond to that of formal channels?
10. What informal social networks are operative during the work day?

11. How active are these networks?
12. How closely do the patterns and hierarchies in informal, social networks correspond to formal organization patterns and hierarchies?
13. What functions do these interactions seem to fulfill?
14. What are the various constituencies (individuals and/or organizations) external to the organization—who exert informal or indirect influence on (or are themselves influenced by) the organization?
15. What individuals within the organization are important to maintaining these interfaces?
16. Of these informal, indirect influences, which have a direct effect on your activities?
17. What are the patterns of informal social relationships outside of work day (parties, tennis, country club, wives, etc.)?
18. How pervasive are these activities?
19. How widespread is involvement?
20. How do patterns and hierarchies in these activities correspond to patterns and hierarchies within the formal structure?
21. What functions do these activities seem to fulfill for participants?

III. Operating Dynamics

1. What leadership styles are utilized within the organization?
2. How are policy decisions made within the organization?
3. How are operating decisions made within the organization?
4. How are decisions ratified (Informally, formally, orally or in written form)?
5. How often are meetings held?
6. Who attends meetings?
7. What is the content of discussion at meetings?
8. What procedures are used in meetings (Parliamentary procedure, informal discussion, etc.)?
9. What formal functions do meetings fulfill?
10. What informal and social functions do meetings fulfill?
11. What furniture arrangements are utilized for meetings?
12. What kinds of meeting environments are selected?
13. Are there consistent seating patterns?
14. What are these patterns?
15. Which of the following roles are utilized?
    Task Oriented Roles:
    (a) *Initiator*—offers new ideas or changed ways of regarding group problems or goals. Suggests solutions—how to handle group difficulty or suggests new procedure for group.
    (b) *Information seeker*—seeks clarification of suggestions in terms of the factual adequacy and/or authoritative information and pertinent facts.
    (c) *Information giver*—offers facts or generalizations which are authoritative or relates own experience pertinently to group problems.
    (d) *Coordinator*—clarifies relationships among ideas and suggestions. Pulls ideas and suggestions together, or tries to coordinate activities of members of sub-groups.
    (e) *Evaluator*—subjects accomplishments of group to "standards" of group functioning. Evaluates or questions practicality, logic, validity, or procedural quality of a suggestion or of some unit of group discussion.
    Relation Oriented Roles:
    (f) *Encourager*—praises, agrees with, and accepts others' ideas. Indicates warmth and solidarity in his attitude toward members.
    (g) *Harmonizer*—mediates intra-group scraps. Relieves tensions.
    (h) *Gatekeeper*—regulates flow of contribution. Encourages and facilitates participation of others.
    (i) *Standard Setter*—articulates standards for group in terms of its quality of relationships within and between members. Applies standards to quality of group processes in light of group objectives.
    (j) *Follower*—goes along passively. Provides friendly audience.

(k) *Group Observer*—stays out of group's proceedings; functions by giving feedback as to what goes on during various phases of meeting.
   Self-oriented Roles:
(l) *Blocker*—tries to meet felt individual needs often at the expense of group. Negativistic. Stubbornly and unreasoningly resistent; tries to bring back into consideration issues group rejected or by-passed.
(m) *Recognition Seeker*—tries to call attention to himself. May boast of accomplishments or personal achievements, and in overdrawn ways. Struggles to prevent being placed in an "inferior" or "one-down" position within group.
(n) *Dominator*—tries to assert authority in manipulating group or some individuals in group. May be flattery, assertion of superior status, giving directions authoritatively, interrupting contributions of others, etc.
(o) *Avoider*—maintains distance from others. Passive resister. Tries to remain insulated from others.

16. By whom are these roles typically employed?
17. Are there consistent patterns of who speaks before and after whom?
18. Are there consistent patterns of who supports whose ideas verbally and non-verbally?
19. Are there consistent patterns of who disagrees with whom?
20. Are there consistent patterns of dominance and submission?
21. Are there consistent patterns of assertion of authority and responses of deference?
22. Who receives most eye contact from the leader?

Discussion

Answers to some of the questions will be easy to obtain. Others will require more thought and research. Some can be answered by asking persons in the organization under study. Others require quiet but thorough observation, and clever information gathering strategies. The process of gathering information is essential to adequate organizational analysis. What are the major implications of the profile? How might the information be useful to a new employee? To a supervisor? To an organizational consultant?

25. Values and Society

This exercise is intended to foster increased awareness of the personal and cultural values characteristic of contemporary society. The activity also provides an opportunity to discuss concepts of culture, societal development, and the role of individual decision-making and values in group concensus. The game requires approximately 45 minutes and may be used with any number of participants.

Procedure

1. Copies of Worksheet 25.1 are distributed to each participant. Five minutes are provided for individuals to read and consider the situation outlined on the worksheet.
2. Participants are asked to take about 10 minutes to decide individually what personal possessions they would take to Alpha III if provided with 100-pound limit.
3. Participants are then grouped in clusters of ten, and told that they have 15 minutes to select those items they wish to take to Alpha III to begin their new society. Their collective limit is 2,500 pounds.
4. After the groups have completed their lists it may be useful to bring all participants together for discussion, or, depending upon the number of individuals involved, at least a portion of the discussion may be conducted within groups.

Worksheet 25.1

ALPHA III

Outside, the skies are orange; all is dead or dying. Your family and friends are dead. The dreaded nuclear war is here. You are one of the ten randomly selected individuals assigned to a spacecraft pre-programmed to depart for the Planet Alpha III. Scientists foresaw the possibility of the total devastation of nuclear war and constructed the underground, lead chamber you are now in. It is stocked with a supply of all the foodstuffs available and a wide range of electronic and technological equipment used in all domains of contemporary human existence. Also, in the chamber are a wide assortment of cultural and artistic items taken from the best museums in the world. Alpha III was selected as the destination for its primitive likeness to Earth. All arrangements have been made for your physical and psychological well-being from the time the spacecraft takes off until the doors open to expose you to the wilderness of Alpha III. In addition to the clothes on your back, each person is allowed to take only 100 pounds of personal possessions. Collectively the individuals may take 2,500 pounds of Earth materials to start and maintain their existence on Alpha III. These materials—both the personal items and the societal ones—must be well chosen, because when the spacecraft departs, no further contact with Earth will be possible.

Discussion

What personal items were selected? What group items were selected? What values and experiences are reflected by the particular personal items selected? What cultural values and social history are reflected in the group's choice of Earth materials? How difficult was it to prepare this list? Why? What was the nature of the group's dynamics during discussion? What leadership patterns emerged? How much agreement was there within the group as to what items should be taken? How were disagreements handled? Did all participants contribute evenly? How did the items selected by different groups compare? Were certain items selected by a number of different groups? How will the new culture that will be developed compare to that on Earth? What are the implications of this for understanding the role of communication in the transmission of culture?

26. Culture I

This activity is designed to simulate aspects of cultural development and evolution, and to underscore dynamics of societal formation and the role of social communication is these phenomena. The exercise requires two or more hours, and can be used with pairs of groups each consisting of 5 to 15 participants.

Procedure

1. Divide participants into even groups of 5 to 15 participants. Each group is assigned a small meeting room and told that no one is to leave the room during the exercise.
2. The instructor distributes a copy of Worksheet 26.1 or 26.2 to each participant.
3. The instructor explains to each group, that they are the passengers of the ill-fated plane which has crashed in the tropical island described on the Worksheet. Unfortunately, there is no hope of rescue. The only chance for survival is to get organized with one another and make the best of the situation and the people in their group.

Worksheet 26.1

CULTURE A

The overseas chartered aircraft which you are aboard develops engine trouble and has to crash land. You have just time to grab your hand luggage and get out before the plane bursts into flames. None of the passengers are hurt, but the pilot did not escape with you. *There is no chance of rescue or escape* because the area in which you find yourself is uninhabited, and the aircraft was well off-course when it crashed.

From the wreckage at the summit of a chain of hills, all that is visible is a sea of waving treetops, occasionally punctuated by a change of color or of height. The land slopes steeply to the east and west and stretches unaltered in all directions to the distant ocean. The sloping floor of the forest is covered with dense underbrush which is intertwined with fast growing vines and creepers. Wet, trailing mosses hang from the branches of the trees and thick lichens and fungi flourish on the trunks. Little sunlight penetrates below the underbrush which is sufficiently dense to impair rapid movement. This thick growth provides shelter for many kinds of birds as is evidenced by the preponderance of noise. The pronounced slopes of the island combined with high humidity and heavy rainfall have caused considerable dissection by streams. On the edges of the banks, sunlight penetrates, and fruit bearing bushes sometimes grow. Where the slope falls away quickly there are rockfalls which have resisted jungle encroachment apart from small bushes and mosses. Here the sun shines and small reptiles are visible on the rocks. Everywhere is the inescapable hum of the insect population which defies even the most diligent swatter. The air is very moist and heavy, yet the clouds promise more rain in the afternoon. Farther down, where the slope is less pronounced, the undergrowth thins until only a canopy of broad-leafed trees shuts out the sunlight and leaves the ground shrouded in mist and darkness.

The groups are each instructed that their task is to plan their strategy for survival. In essence they will each be involved in the development of a society and a culture that will support their group's survival in the alien land. They must make decisions about division of *labor, governance, living accommodations, economics, laws, sex roles, values,* etc., with the goal of developing the sort of society that will meet their personal and social needs while at the same time insuring their biological well-being.
4. The instructor informs each group that he or she will provide cues to them periodically to indicate how much time has passed since their plane crashed. Additionally, the instructor will ask questions from time to time to facilitate the groups' planning and development of their society.
5. After 20 minutes, the instructor asks each group what their society is like at the end of three days? Twenty minutes later, participants are asked what the society is like at the end of a month? After an additional ten minutes have elapsed, they are asked how their society appears after six months. Participants are asked to indicate individually what they are doing in the society after six months. What roles does each participant have in the society? How does he or she feel about the society? Its members? Its laws? Its values?

Worksheet 26.2

CULTURE B

The overseas chartered aircraft which you are aboard, develops engine trouble and has to crash land. You have just time to grab your hand luggage and get out before the plane bursts into flames. None of the passengers are hurt but the pilot did not escape with you. *There is no chance of rescue or escape* because the area in which you find yourself is uninhabited, and the aircraft was well off-course when it crashed.

The breakers pulverize the stricken aircraft as the incoming tide covers the mudflat where the forced landing was made. Beyond the reach of the waves stretch the reeds and grasses of a bog. As the land rises, the bog turns to meadow and at the summit of the hill rise a few tortured, flat-topped trees. The island is low and wind swept as is evidenced by the dunes above the swamp. As the elevation increases, sea cliffs rise until the island falls abruptly to the sea. It appears to be about 10 miles long at its greatest point. No natural source of fresh water is visible. Animal life consists mainly of birds and smaller mammals including rabbits and mice. In addition, signs of wild goats are seen. In the shallower waters where the wrecked plane lies there are shell fish and small sharks which make wading hazardous. Below the cliffs the waves are broken by smashed rock and debris which foretell severe battering by both wind and waves. The air is warm and very dry telling of a long period of drought, as does the brownness of the grass and trees on the hillside. Rainless clouds scud across the horizon which is completely flat, bearing signs of neither land nor life.

After another twenty minutes have passed, participants are asked to consider what their society will be like at the end of one year; at the end of five, ten and twenty years? Encourage them to plan their society as carefully and appropriately as possible; they have a unique opportunity to construct the ideal society with the ideal culture.
6. Following completion of the long-run development phase of the societal simulation, proceed with discussion. If at all possible, separate the groups for discussion, particularly if the instructor wishes to follow this exercise with *Culture II*.

Discussion

What happened? How effectively did each group operate within the exercise? How adequate was the society and culture they developed? Was the society the best one for the particular environment? What kind of society was developed? What were its strengths? Its weaknesses? What kind of culture resulted? What work roles were assigned? What values were emphasized? What governance structures were established? Sexual practices? Leisure practices? Religious practices? Economic systems? What about criminal justice systems? etc. Did the society evenly reflect the needs and desires of all members of the group? Were there dissident factions? How were differing views accommodated? In what respects did the processes which occurred in the exercise parallel real-life societal development processes? In what respects were the group dynamics within the society like those in everyday communication situations? What leadership patterns developed within the group? How closely did the society and its values parallel those of Western cultures? What were the major similarities? Major differences?

PART 3
CROSS-CULTURAL AND INTERCULTURAL COMMUNICATION

Cross-cultural or intercultural communication is two or more persons with different backgrounds, sending and receiving messages and endeavoring to coordinate their meanings. The basic process is not unique to cross-cultural communication. In many respects all aspects of cross-cultural communication are present any time two persons talk and listen to one another.

Even when two people from one cultural background attempt to interact with one another, the process is complex, and only partial coordination of meaning is possible. Each person speaks from his or her own frame of reference, which reflects a particular set of life experiences that are to some extent unique for each person. When I speak to you, the words I select have meanings for me which have been shaped directly by my education, my family experiences, language, customs, geographical heritage, political and religious orientations, and so on. What you hear and understand is never exactly what I mean. In effect, you hear in terms of your own communicative frame of reference. The words I use, you interpret in terms of your education, family experiences, language, customs, geographical heritage, religious and political background, and so on.

If we were sending messages to one another in a face-to-face context, not only our words, but also our pace of speaking, gestures, body positions, and dress are also part of the messages we send to one another, consciously, but more often not. Depending largely upon how similar our past experiences have been, we may have greater or less ease in understanding the words and gestures we are using, in a similar way.

Culture is a term which we can use loosely here to denote in aggregate, the factors which provide the basis for what we generally think of as past experience. Thus, to say two people are from one culture is to suggest that they're likely to commonly share some things, perhaps language, geographical and economic orientation, for example.

When we speak of communication between persons within or from one culture—intracultural communication—we are speaking of communication between persons who may have many things in common. This improves the likelihood that each may understand the other's messages—words and actions—somewhat as the other intends. Figure (A) depicts this relationship visually. The circles represent the communication frameworks of two persons from the same culture, and the area of overlap represents the degree to which their communicative frameworks are similar.

**Figure (A)
A Model of Relationships**

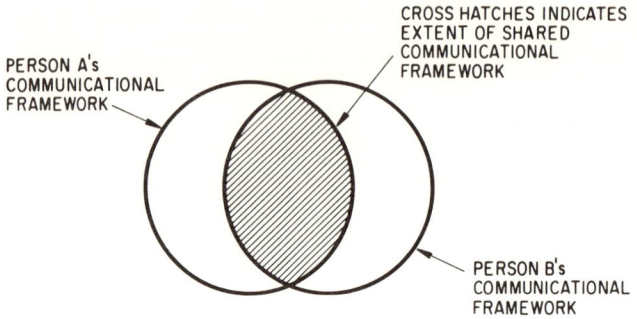

Even among persons who may have spent much time together within a single culture, such as brothers and sisters, husbands and wives, or good friends, the circles would not overlap totally. Each individual retains a communicational framework that will to some extent remain unique, reflecting his or her individualized experiences, desires, successes and failures, needs, aspirations, etc. It is useful to understand how, even within one culture, relationships may progress from first acquaintance (depicted in the first of the three graphs) through stages of increasing overlap of communicational framework (center), to relatively well developed areas of mutuality (right).

**Figure (B)
The Progression of Relationships**

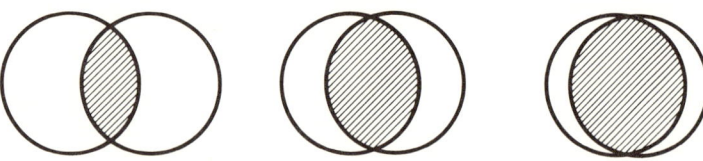

If we take this same approach to thinking about cross-cultural communication—the sending and receiving of messages between two persons from different cultures—the circles will likely range somewhere between the extremes depicted in Figure (C), depending upon the extent of differences in language, customs, political, religious, and geographical orientation.

Thus, an interaction between French-speaking and English-speaking Canadians, provides an example of cross-cultural communication which falls toward the extreme depicted on the left. In these examples, there are differences in communicational frameworks, in terms of geographical factors and to some extent, customs. These disparaties, however, are quite small compared to those present in efforts at interaction between a North American, and an African or Asian, for example, which illustrates the sort of cross-cultural relationship depicted in the drawing to the right.

Figure (C)
The Range of Cross-cultural Relationships

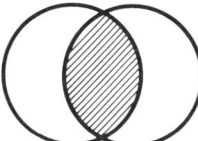 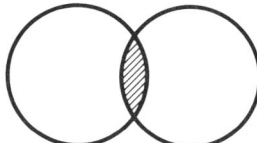

In the former case, the interaction between the U.S. citizen and the English-speaking Canadian, the American begins to understand that when he hears the phrase "on the odd day," the meaning is more like "on the occasional day" than it is "on the strange day," which would be the more typical meaning in the States. And, there may be differences in communication styles between each set of partners which are to some degree characteristic of the respective cultural influences.

Characterizing the other extreme are efforts to negotiate meanings among two persons who may lack a common language, customs, political, religious, and economic orientations, and who may have radically different orientations to time, space, physical contact, verbal pace and other non-verbal communication factors.

The exercises in this section of the volume focus on cultural development, cross-cultural interaction, cultural intervention, international development, inter-racial and international values, cross-cultural bargaining and negotiation, cross-cultural effectiveness, language and cross-cultural communication. Included also are case studies which deal with aspects of cross-cultural communication, adjustment, and development.

Bibliography

Chu, Y. K., "Introduction to Cross-cultural Learning," in S. Fersh (Ed.), *Learning About Peoples and Cultures,* Evanston, Ill.: McDougal, Little, Co., 1974.

Fersh, S., "Semantics and the Study of Cultures," in S. Fersh (Ed.), *Learning About Peoples and Cultures,* Evanston, Ill.: McDougal, Little, Co., 1974.

Kunkhiro, M., "Language in Intercultural Communication," in S. Fersh (Ed.), *Learning About Peoples and Cultures,* Evanston, Ill.: McDougal, Little, Co., 1974.

Samovar, L. A., and Porter, R. W., *Intercultural Communication: A Reader,* Belmont, Calif.: Wadsworth, 1972.

Sarbaugh, L., *Intercultural Communication,* Rochelle Park, N.J.: Hayden, (in press).

27. Culture II

This exercise is intended as an optional follow-up sequence to *Culture I*. It provides participants a sense of the culture-bound nature of perception, values, ethics, and behavior. Additionally, it highlights aspects of cross-cultural communication. Culture II requires approximately 1½ to 2 hours for completion, and can be used with pairs of groups consisting of 5 to 15 participants each.

Procedure

1. Separate participants such that each group of 5 to 15 persons occupies a separate small room. It is desirable to retain the same groups as those developed in *Culture I*. Each group is reminded that a full twenty years have passed since the tragic air crash confined them to their island existence (See Worksheet 26.1 or 26.2).
2. Each group is advised that a message has just been found on the shore. It is believed that the message was delivered to the island by a lone courier in a handmade outrigger. The message indicates that another society exists on an adjacent island about 10 miles away. Apparently, this society was also formed by a group of individuals who were the survivors of an airplane crash which took place some twenty years ago. The instructor informs the group that the message indicates that the other society is urging an exchange of visitors between one another's society. The goal is to get to know one another's culture better, and to consider ways the two societies might help one another.
3. The instructor informs members of each group that they have fifteen minutes to prepare for their first exchange with the other society. During this time period, they are asked to select one person from their society who will visit the other culture. They may wish to brief their emissary during the time remaining after his or her selection.
4. Toward the end of the 15 minute period, the instructor advises each group that henceforth they will be referred to as the green (or blue) culture. One group in every pair of groups is labeled green, the other blue.
5. The green culture representative and the blue culture representative are directed by the instructor to the rooms housing the other's culture. The following instructions are then read in turn, to each culture and the visiting emissary: "Mr. (or Ms.) _____ will be visiting your culture for 10 minutes. Because time is limited, you will no doubt want to acquaint him or her with the basics of the green (or blue) culture as rapidly as possible, so that he or she can fairly represent the green (or blue) culture to his (or her) own society. You may use the 10 minutes in any manner you wish."
6. At the end of the 10-minute period, emissaries return to their home culture and are provided with 15 minutes to discuss the exchange.

7. Following this discussion, the instructor announces that word from the other culture is that they would like to continue the cultural exchange program, and that a series of visits—one visit per group member—are to take place during which the two cultures will further explore differences and similarities with the goal of identifying areas of mutual interest.

   Both cultures are informed they will have 10 minutes to determine those areas where they lack comprehensive information regarding the other culture. They are to focus on those concerns they believe are necessary in order to decide whether the two societies are likely to benefit from further intercultural exchange. Each group prepares a list of topical inquiry areas: governance, verbal and non-verbal styles, economics, sex practices, work-leisure patterns, religious practices, values, etc., are examples. Each culture also selects one of its members to focus upon each topic area.
8. A series of intercultural exchanges are conducted for a duration of 5 minutes each. The purpose is to enable the representatives of each culture to gather information about his or her topical area of inquiry.
9. Approximately two minutes are provided between each of these exchanges, for minimal briefing and debriefing of the representatives by their respective cultures.
10. After each member of both the green and blue society has had an opportunity to visit the other culture, the instructor announces that an official communique has been received from the other culture suggesting that the two merge to form a larger society composed of both the green and blue culture. Each group is asked to carefully consider the proposal, drawing fully upon the information gathered during cultural exchange and to reach a decision. Ten to fifteen minutes are provided for these deliberations.

Discussion

Depending upon the number of participants involved and the purposes of the instructor, discussion of the exercise might be conducted either with members of both green and blue cultures together, or with each separately.

What decision did participants think the other culture reached? Why? How would you characterize the blue culture? The green culture? What were the major differences? How receptive was each society to the intercultural exchange program? Were any differences between the two cultures obvious in the way you were received during your visit? Did the blue culture develop a clear identity of its own? Did the green culture develop a clear identity? Were any difficulties in "intercultural communication" encountered? Did "culture shock" take place? To what extent were individual participants "brainwashed" to accept the values and behavioral norms of their own cultures? How difficult was it for participants to consider the perspective of the other culture? How does this experience relate to problems of cultural exchange in the international context? What are the values of cultural exchange? Are there dysfunctions of cultural exchange? How does this exercise pertain to intercultural communication problems as they occur in the "real world?"

28. Culture III

This exercise can be used as a follow-up to *Culture I*, or subsequent to *Culture II*. It can also be used without previous *Culture* sequences. The activity focuses on the dimensions of trust, competition, and negotiation, in an intercultural communication context. The game can be used with pairs of groups consisting of 5–15 participants each.

Procedure

1. The instructor or facilitator organizes participants into two (or multiple pairs) of 5 to 15 participants, each of which is assigned to a separate small room. If used as a sequel to *Culture I* or *II*, it is desirable to retain the same groupings.
2. Each group is informed by the instructor that a full twenty-five years have passed since their plane crashed and condemned them to their island existence. (See Worksheets 26.1 or 26.2.)
3. The instructor explains to each group that a message has been found on the shore. It is believed, participants are told, that the message was delivered to the island by a courier in a handmade outrigger. The communique indicates that another society was also formed by a group of individuals who were survivors of an airplane crash which occurred nearly twenty-five years ago. The message indicates that the other society is near starvation and wishes to explore the possibility of securing help; suggesting a unique exploratory system of communication between the two cultures. The plan calls for each culture to enter into interaction with one another for ten message exchanges.
4. One group is designated the Green Culture; the other the Blue Culture.
5. The Cultures are told that during each of the ten exchanges, the two cultures will interact using a unique "language." Green Culture will either send an "A" message or a "B" message. Blue Culture will send an "X" or "Y" message.
6. The choice of one letter of the other (A or B for Green, X or Y for Blue) will be made by each Culture on a round by round basis, for each of 10 rounds.
7. Participants are informed that the various combinations of choices result in the following point assignments for the cultures.

Message Choices		Survival Points	
Green Culture	Blue Culture	Green Culture	Blue Culture
A	X	+5	+5
A	Y	−10	+10
B	X	+10	−10
B	Y	−5	−5

8. The instructor explains to both cultures that *Survival Points* are accumulated by each culture, during each of the ten rounds of communication. Both cultures are also informed that if either culture fails to get at least 25 *Survival Points,* it is assumed that that culture will be destroyed by starvation. In the event that neither culture earns at least 25 points, both will be destroyed.
9. The instructor signals the beginning of Round 1, instructing each culture that it has three minutes to determine whether they wish to send an A or B message (in the case of the Green Culture; or an X or Y for the Blue Culture). At the end of the round, the instructor directs each group to indicate its decision on a piece of paper, which he or she collects at the same time.
10. The instructor announces each decision to the other culture, and posts the resultant scores on a blackboard or flip chart labeled "Communication Tally Sheet."
11. Rounds 2 and 3 are conducted in the same manner, with three minutes each, and scores posted after each round.
12. Before beginning Round 4, the instructor points out that each culture may elect to send an emissary to meet with a representative from the other culture, to discuss matters of mutual interest. Allow approximately five minutes for each culture to determine whether they will send a representative, and for deciding who the representative will be, if they so opt.
13. Allow 5 minutes for the two emissaries to confer.
14. When emissaries have returned to their respective cultures, an additional five minutes is allowed for each culture to reach a decision as to which message it will send in Round 4. Scores are posted in the usual manner, and the two cultures begin Round 5 deliberations.
15. Rounds 6, 7, and 8 proceed without interaction between emissaries; three minutes are provided for each round.
16. Prior to Round 9, another, optional five-minute negotiation session is provided for emissaries to confer. The same or different persons may be selected as emissaries. Following a five minute conference, representatives return to their respective cultures, for an additional five minute discussion as to which message the culture will send.
17. Round 9 scores are posted, and Round 10 proceeds in the normal manner, again with three minutes for discussion.

Discussion

Discussion may be conducted in one of several formats: With each group separately, with both groups together, or a combination thereof. It is sometimes useful to precede discussion by asking each group to spend ten minutes answering the following questions: Who won? Why do you conclude this? What were your culture's motives during the message sending? What do you believe were the motives of the other culture? After these questions are answered, it may be useful, depending upon one's purposes, to bring the cultures together and ask each, in turn, to review their answers to these questions. Often because of differences in assessments of who won, and assumptions as to motives, animated discussion can be generated. In this regard, it is often useful in the total group to consider at some length each of the above questions. For example, there are various definitions of winning—economic victories, moral victories, etc.—that one might select. Of course, each has different implications for determination of the winning culture.

It is also important to facilitate a discussion of the dynamics underlying a group's determination of its definitions of winning. At what point did particular definitions emerge? Were decisions to strive for "moral victory" determined before or after chances for an economic one seemed slim?

What values operated within each culture during the activity? Competitiveness? Cooperativeness? How were decisions made? What leadership patterns emerged? Were these dynamics consistent with the stated values of the culture? Were the same values that were applied to members of one's own culture utilized in dealings with the other culture? Which aspects of this activity have applicability in thinking about intercultural and international dynamics in the "real world?" Are there possible lessons to be drawn from this activity that have implications for cross-cultural and international relations?

29. Cross-Cultural Communication Guide

The self-instructional guide to cross-cultural communication is a structured information-gathering inventory designed to lead users to some important aspects of effective cross-cultural communication. The profile can be completed individually or through group activity, and may require as little as an hour to as much as several weeks to complete, depending upon instructional objectives.

Procedure

1. Distribute copies of the self-instructional guide to cross-cultural communication, provided in the Cross-Cultural Communication Guide. See Worksheet 29.1.
2. Participants may gather information individually or in groups, depending upon the instructor's objectives.
3. Participants compare completed worksheets and discuss the various information-gathering strategies they utilized.
4. It may also be useful to identify and discuss any areas of importance which are not covered by the guide, and to consider whether some of the questions in the guide reflect western cultural biases.

Worksheet 29.1

SELF-TAUGHT GUIDE: A CROSS-CULTURAL COMMUNICATION QUESTIONNAIRE

A. Social Customs

1. Are the people overtly friendly, reserved and formal, or hostile to strangers?
2. What are formal and informal greeting forms? Which may be used appropriately by a guest? by a child?
3. What are appropriate manners for entering a house? (Do you remove your shoes or any other items of clothing before entering? Do you wait to be welcomed in by the owner or await the owner inside the door? Do you send a calling card in advance? Do you ring a bell, clap hands, or bang with your fist on the floor?)
4. What are appropriate manners when shopping? In a bazaar? In a salon or store? (Do you call for a salesperson or wait until a clerk approaches you? Do you bargain? Are you expected to carry your purchases? Do you provide your own containers for food purchases?)
5. What are appropriate manners at the theatre? (Do you clap hands or shout "bravo" or hiss or whistle to show approval? Do you seat yourself or await an usher? Do you tip the usher? How do you get a program?)
6. What are appropriate manners in a beauty shop? (Do you make an appointment in advance or walk in? Do you bring your own beauty supplies? To whom do you give tips?)
7. What are appropriate manners for entering a room? (Do you bow, nod, or shake hands with others there? Do you shake hands with everyone, only males, no one, or only the first person to greet you?)

8. What is the appropriate moment in a new relationship to give one's name, ask the other's name, inquire about occupation or family? How are names used for introductions? (When compound names are customary, which elements do you use?) How do you present Sra. Maria Josefina Molina de Diez de Medina or Senorita Consuelo Vazquez Qutierrez de Arr?
9. Is it proper for a wife to show affection for her husband in public by a term of endearment, holding his hand, or greeting him with a kiss?
10. What is the expected gesture of appreciation for an invitation to a home? (Do you bring a gift, what kind? Do you send flowers in advance, after? Do you send a thank-you note?)
11. When gifts are exchanged, is it impolite to open the gift in the presence of the donor? Are gifts presented or received in a special manner? Is it proper to express appreciation for a gift? Are any gift items taboo?
12. Are there any customs affecting the way one sits or where one sits? (Is it impolite to sit with feet pointed toward another person? Is the right of the host a position of special honor?)
13. What are the ways of showing respect (hat off or on, sitting or standing, bowing, lowering head, etc.?)
14. Are there special observances a guest should be familiar with before attending a wedding, funeral, baptism, birthday, or official ceremony?
15. Is it offensive to put your hand on the arm of someone with whom you are talking?
16. Do you offer your arm when escorting someone across the street?
17. What are reactions to laughing, crying, fainting, or blushing in a group situation?
18. Are any particular facial expressions or gestures considered rude?
19. Do people tend to stand more closely when talking? What is the concept of proper personal space?
20. What constitute "personal" questions?
21. What is the attitude toward punctuality for social and business appointments?
22. How do you politely attract the attention of a waiter in a restaurant?
23. How can invitations be refused without causing offense? Is a previous engagement an acceptable excuse? What happens if the excuse of illness is used?

B. Family Life

1. What is the basic unit of social organization—the individual, the basic family, the extended family, the tribe, the village, the region, the linguistic group, the national state?
2. What family members of which generations live together? If you are invited to a home, whom in the family would you expect to meet?
3. Are the elderly treated with special respect? Are they greeted differently from other adults? Does a young person look forward to or dread old age?
4. Is homemaking considered the preferred role for women? How do women figure in the labor force, the professions, officialdom?
5. What are the duties in the family of women, of men? Who controls the family money? Who makes the decision about the upbringing of children?
6. How do the inheritance laws work? Can female offspring inherit land? Does the last born have a different legacy from the first born? What arrangements are usual for widows?
7. What do girls aspire to become? What careers are preferred for boys? Do toys and games ascribe special roles to either sex?
8. How are children taught (by rote, by precept, by conceptual learning)? Who are his teachers in and out of school? What techniques are used at home and at school to reinforce desirable behavior and to correct disapproved behavior?
9. What are the important events in family life and how are they celebrated?
10. When does a child become an adult and is there a ceremony to mark passage from one stage to the next? (Debutante ball, circumcision rites, Bar Mitzvah?)
11. Are marriages planned or by individual choice? What do people look for or want from marriage? Who pays for the wedding ceremony? Is a dowry necessary?
12. At what age do most marry: What encounters between the sexes are approved prior to marriage? Is chastity a virtue? Is polygamy or concubinage approved? Is homosexuality accepted?

13. Is divorce permitted?
14. What are the symbols used in the marriage ceremony and what do they signify?

C. Housing, Clothing, and Food

1. What functions are served by the average dwelling? Is there a separate structure for performing ablutions, cooking, keeping of animals, or storage of foodstuffs?
2. Are there differences in the kind of housing used by different social groups? Differences in location, type of building or furnishings?
3. Which textiles, colors, or decorations are identified with specific social or occupational groups and considered appropriate for others? (Special colors for royalty, for mourning.)
4. What occasions require special dress, foods (for holidays, religious events)?
5. Are there some types of clothing considered taboo for one or the other sex?
6. What parts of the body must always be covered by clothing?
7. How many meals a day are customary?
8. With what implements is food eaten? In a common bowl or individual servings? Is there an age or sex separation at meal times? Is there a special role for hosts and guests in regard to who eats where, what and when? Are there any customary expectations about the amount of food guests must be offered or must eat? Any special rituals for drinking?
9. Are there any foods unique to the country not eaten elsewhere?
10. Which foods are of importance for ceremonies and festivals?
11. Which are the prestige foods? (Champaigne and caviar equivalents)
12. What types of eating places, what sorts of food and drink are indicative of appropriate hospitality for: a) relatives; b) close friends; c) official acquaintances; and d) strangers?
13. Is "setting a good table" important for social recognition?
14. When dining, where is the seat of honor?

D. Class Structure

1. Into what classes is society organized? (Royalty, aristocracy, large landowners, industrialists, military, artists, professionals, merchants, artisans, industrial workers, small farm owners, farm laborers, etc.)
2. Are there racial, religious, or economic factors which determine social status? Are there any minority groups? What is their social standing? Is wealth a prerequisite for public office?
3. Does birth predetermine status?
4. Is class structure in rural areas different from that of urban areas?
5. Is there a group of individuals or families who occupy a pre-dominant social position? Can they easily be identified? Is their status attributable to heredity, money, land or political influence?
6. Are there any particular roles or activities appropriate (or inappropriate) to the status in which expatriates are classified? (Does high status imply facility for generous contributions to charitable causes? Does a man lose great face by helping his wife with dishes or changing diapers?)

E. Political Patterns

1. Are there immediate outside threats to the political survival of the country? What protections does the country have against any such threats? What defensive alliances? What technological advantages in weaponry? What traditional enemies that color policy options?
2. How is political power manifested? (Through traditional institutions of government, through control of the military, through economic strength?)
3. What channels are open for the expression of popular opinion?
4. What media of information are important? Who controls them? Who do they reach? What are the sources of information available to the average citizen?
5. What are the political structures for the cities? (Mayors, councils?) and for the countryside? (village chiefs, town councils?)

6. How is international representation handled? What is the process for formulating foreign policy? Who receives visiting heads of state? Who negotiates treaties?
7. If a profile of the power structure should be drawn, which individuals or groups, visible or "behind the scenes," would figure as key elements?
8. In social situations, who talks politics? Is it a subject in which a guest may show interest?
9. What channels, if any, are available to opposition groups to express dissent?

F. Religion and Folk Beliefs

1. To which religious groups do people belong? Is one predominant?
2. How can the fundamental religious beliefs be described?
3. Are there any religious beliefs which influence daily activities? (noon prayers, begging bowls?)
4. Is religion institutionalized? What is the hierarchy of religious functionaries, and in what ways do they interact with the people?
5. Which places have sacred value? Which objects? Which events and festivals? Which writings?
6. Is there tolerance for minority religions? (Is proselytizing or educational activities of minority religions permitted?)
7. What is said or done to exorcise evil spirits (knocking on wood, making the sign of the cross?)
8. What is done with a new child or enterprise or building to insure good fortune?
9. What objects or actions portend good luck, which bad luck?
10. What myths are taught to children as part of their cultural heritage (sandman, Jack Frost, Père Noel, fairy godmother, Santa Claus, etc.)?

G. Economic Institutions

1. How do the geographic location and climate affect the ways food, clothing and shelter are provided? (Has extensive irrigation or hydro-electric development been necessary? Has terrain facilitated or obstructed development of air transport?)
2. How adequate are the available natural resources? Which must be imported? Which are in sufficient supply to be exported?
3. What foodstuffs, if any, must the country import?
4. What are the principal products? Major exports? Imports? What is the GNP?
5. In the market places, what items basic to a minimum standard of living do you find missing? Are luxury items available?
6. What kinds of technological training are offered?
7. Are industrial workers organized in unions, confederations, political parties or none of these? What about rural workers?
8. Are cooperatives important in the economy?
9. Are businesses generally of the family type or large public corporation or government-operated? Is the multinational corporation significant?
10. What percent of the population is engaged in agriculture, in industry, in service trades?
11. What protections have been developed against natural disasters? (Floating construction to minimize earthquake damage, advanced warning systems for typhoons, extensive crop insurance backed by the government, private disaster relief?)

H. Arts

1. Which media for artistic expression are most esteemed?
2. Are there professional artists? Art schools?
3. Which materials are most used? Stone, ivory, bone, shell, wood, clay, metal, reed, textile, glass?
4. What art objects would you find?

I. Value Systems

1. Is life to be enjoyed or viewed as a source of suffering?

2. Is competitiveness or cooperativeness most prized?
3. Is thrift, or enjoyment of the moment, more exalted?
4. Is work viewed as an end in itself or as a necessary output to be kept to a minimum?
5. Is *face* considered more important than *fact*?
6. Is politeness regarded as more important than factual honesty?
7. What killing, if any, is sanctioned? (Capital punishment, war, killing of adulterer, infanticide during famine?)
8. How is *friend* defined? What are the responsibilities of friendship?
9. What are the injunctions taught children?
10. Who are the traditional heroes or heroines? From what field of endeavor? Who are the popular idols of the day? What values do they symbolize?
11. How would the virtues and vices be defined?
12. How would work as compared to play be defined?

Discussion

A number of approaches to the questionnaire are possible. One may choose to discuss just one aspect of the cross-cultural relationship, such as the importance or influence of social class in various cultures. For example, one might exchange ideas on how social status is achieved in these societies, and what are the symbols of status, both high and low? Does high social status imply economic power or have any bearing on political advancement? Is social status affected by race or religion?

A number of approaches to the questionnaire are possible. One may choose to focus on a single area of study. For example, how in this other culture, is social status achieved. What are the symbols of status, high and low? Does high social status imply economic power or have any bearing on political influence? Is social status affected by race or religion?

Or, one may centrally examine the importance of symbols of all kinds. What is the significance of the dragon in folk art of the country? Why are cattle blessed, or fishing vessels launched on a certain date? Why bring bread and salt to a housewarming? A wealth of information can be mined by probing behind the facade of ceremonies, superstitions, and the use of certain patterns or forms in art.

The focus in language offers another rich approach to intercultural study. What are popular sayings and what attitudes do they reveal? What is the role of women in a country with the adage "A woman and a calendar are good for only one year?"

Also fruitful is the pursuit of the meaning behind abstract terms. How, for example, are the words "democracy" or "socialism" used? What does it mean to different elements within the society? Does the designation "efficient" imply a compliment or criticism?

Or one might similarly discuss the cross-cultural dimension of arts and crafts. One can examine the importance of symbols in art forms, particularly the folk art of the countries concerned. A wealth of information can be obtained by diligently probing behind the facade of ceremonies, superstitions and the use of non-verbal communication.

On the other hand, one can investigate the extent to which Western concepts or assumptions have influenced the make-up and bias of the Questionnaire itself. Some samples of these "Western" biases which are inherently conspicuous in Western thinking and philosophy, and to which participants should be sensitive, include the following:

(a) *Action is Good:* Generally, westerners believe man can induce change through individual action. "Getting things done" is commendable; "doing" is more important than "being" or "becoming."

(b) *Man's Environment Can Be Controlled:* Nature is something to be conquered and its forces harnessed to man's needs. Actively attacking problems of natural environment, such as climate, topography, space, etc., is regarded as inspiring.

(c) *Progress is Upward and not a Spiral:* In Western cultures, change is regarded as an inevitable part of life. Decisions are made in anticipation of the future. Utopia lies ahead on the road to progress.

(d) *The Material is more real than the Spiritual:* In the Western cultures things that are tangible and measurable are valued.

(e) *Every Man makes His own Success Or Is Responsible For His Own Failure:* Self-esteem in the West is closely tied to one's personal success and a "natural" desire to get ahead. This leads to a competitive way of life, and the desire to improve social status through personal efforts. Compare this philosophy of life with that of India, which preaches the doctrine of "karma," in which man is already pre-destined to a way of life as a result of his conduct in a previous birth.

(f) *Individual Responsibility Is Thought To Be Very Important.* Group action is encouraged, but ultimately the individual is held to be the cornerstone of society. The individual is protected by certain inalienable rights, which are guaranteed by the Constitution.

One has to be particularly aware of these manifestations of "Western" concepts or biases by which other cultures are judged. Strong influences of the above-mentioned values can be found in the Questionnaire.

Other questions worth discussing as a result of the completed Questionnaire would be finding out what values operated within each culture—competitiveness or cooperativeness? Were the same values applied to the members of one's own culture or utilized in dealings with the other culture?

The discussion should also contain an exhaustive checklist of resource materials that were researched for the Questionnaire's completion, and the strategies involved to obtain all this data.

And perhaps the discussion would be somewhat more complete if participants could identify and discuss any areas of importance which are not covered by the Questionnaire.

30. Cross-Cultural Effectiveness

This exercise is designed to focus upon dimensions of intercultural effectiveness, and to provide a basis for exploring the problems individuals encounter in cross-cultural efforts. The exercise also provides the raw material for exploring the dynamics of individual and group decision-making. The activity requires approximately 45 minutes and can be used with groups of 5 to 10 persons.

Procedure
1. Distribute one copy of Worksheet 30.1 to each participant.
2. Ask each individual to read and carefully consider the statements provided on the worksheet.

Worksheet 30.1

CROSS-CULTURAL EFFECTIVENESS

_____ The work-related competence of an individual is the most critical factor in his or her success in cross-cultural tasks.

_____ One's awareness of himself, his own culture, and his styles of communication are critical to effectiveness in a cross-cultural setting.

_____ Especially where an individual is involved in a work-role with other persons, his or her ability to work with members of the work group is probably the most essential factor to effectiveness in a new culture.

_____ An awareness of the cultural, political, and economic realities of the country or culture in which an individual is operating is clearly most essential to effective functioning.

_____ One's ability to tolerate new and ambiguous situations is the most critical factor in effective functioning in a differing culture.

_____ Husband-wife and family relations are the groundwork on which satisfactory cross-cultural functioning is built, without them it is impossible for individuals to operate either efficiently or effectively.

_____ Fitting comfortably with other individuals who are also strangers to a new culture provides the support system one needs to adapt to and function effectively in any new environment. These relations are likely the most critical factor in a cross-cultural environment.

_____ The happiness of spouse and family members in the new culture is critical. Whether their happiness involves comfortable placement in schools or finding meaningful employment of leisure activities, one's effectiveness in a task-role in a new culture depends first and foremost upon the members of the family feeling comfortable.

---

3. Without consulting others, each individual ranks the statements in order of agreement. Participants place a "1" next to the statement with which they most agree, a "2" by the one they most agree with next, etc.

4. After all participants have completed their own individual rankings, the group is given the task of arriving at one overall ranking.
5. This group decision-making process can proceed in whatever manner the group members select.

Discussion

The dimensions of cross-cultural adaptation included in this exercise are those frequently mentioned among the criteria for success in a new culture. There are differences of opinion as to which are most important. Clearly, all contribute to the total impact an individual is likely to have, and their weighting is likely a consequence of the particular situation in which one is placed. The major value of the exercise is thus to acquaint participants with these conditions and the variety of views that may be expressed relative to the importance of each.

The discussion process itself, also becomes a useful focus, and the dynamics of small group interaction and decision-making and persuasion, in general, can be explored. Which methods of decision-making were most effective? What leadership styles predominated? How representative of the individual preferences is the final group ranking? Were some group members more persuasive than others? Why? Additional dimensions of focus are suggested through the use of communication process observation forms.

31. Cultural Intervention

This exercise is designed to focus upon dimensions of cultural development, and to provide a means for exploring the dynamics of individual and group decision-making. The activity requires approximately 45 minutes and can be used with groups of 5 to 10 persons. Each group of participants should be seated in a circle or around a table.

Procedure

1. Distribute one copy of Worksheet 31.1 to each participant.

Worksheet 31.1

GOALS OF CROSS-CULTURAL INTERVENTION

_____The world community will exist as a whole only to the extent that individuals of diverse background accept universal standards of appropriate human behavior. Intentionally, or not, the development of these standards of acceptable behavior is the ultimate goal of cultural intervention.

_____The highest peak of human existence is characterized by a man performing skillfully in a job he or she sincerely enjoys. The primary goal of cultural intervention should be helping individuals become matched with the right job.

_____Cross-cultural interaction should be valued for its own sake simply because in exchange there is growth.

_____The solidarity of the family unit is of crucial importance to the stability of the individual and society alike. Cultural intervention should be aimed at insuring the continuity of the basic family unit.

_____Because it is essential to the survival of mankind that various cultures work with one another, the goal of cultural intervention should be to teach us first and foremost to be informed, reliable, and cooperative members of the world community.

_____Notwithstanding all the rhetoric, one must acknowledge that it is natural for man to want a reasonably comfortable way of life and a share of good things. Cultural intervention should primarily be directed to bring recipients money and positions they value.

_____The primary though seldom acknowledged goal of cross-cultural intervention is the personal growth and development of individuals sent to other cultures.

_____If our culture is to advance, it must be done in the knowledge of the differences which exist between ours and other cultures. Cultural intervention should strive to enable participants from our culture to identify aspects of other cultures and life styles to be avoided, as well as those to be adopted in our own country.

_____The ultimate goal of cultural intervention is freedom of choice. Persons with little knowledge of countries other than their own, are often not able to make intelligent choices in some important areas of life. The goal of intervention is to raise the level of information and alternatives available.

_____The primary goal of cultural intervention is to benefit the country or culture sponsoring the intervention. Realistically, it would be nonsensical to encourage aid or other planned intervention were there no benefit to the donor culture.

2. Ask each individual to read and carefully consider the statements provided on the worksheet.
3. Without consulting others, each individual ranks the statements in order of agreement. Participants place a "1" next to the statement with which they most agree, a "2" by the one they most agree with next, etc.
4. After all group members have completed their own individual rankings, the group is given the task of arriving at one overall ranking, from 1 to 10.
5. This group decision-making proceeds in whatever manner the group members select; voting may not be used as the sole basis for determining the order. Similarly arithmetic averaging of the individual ranks is permitted to be used if accompanied by discussion of the items.

Discussion

The statements included in the exercise represent the spectrum of sentiment on the goals, consequences, and functions of cross-cultural intervention. Clearly, there are necessarily no right or wrong answers. As such, it is useful to focus discussion on the process of group decision-making, as well as on the substance of the statements that the group sought to rank. What methods did the group use in its attempts at consensus? Which methods were most effective? How representative of the individual preferences is the overall group ranking? Were some group members more successful at influencing the group than others. (One way to gather information on this question is to ask all participants to add up the differences between their personal scores and the overall group score across all statements. The smaller the "difference score," the closer the individual was to the ultimate group rank). What kinds of leadership were present in the decision-making process? Democratic? Authoritarian? Was the leadership effective? Did all members participate equally in the decision-making? How well does the final ranking represent individuals in the group? How well did the group tolerate opinions which were not consistent with the majority? Additional dimensions may be usefully underscored through the use of process observation guides.

32. Inter-racial, Intercultural, and International Values

This exercise is designed to focus upon cross-cultural values. The activity requires approximately 45 minutes and can be used with groups of 5–50 persons. Each group of participants should be seated in a circle or around a table.

Procedure

1. Distribute one copy of Worksheet 32.1 to each participant.
2. Ask each individual to read and carefully consider the statements provided on the worksheet.
3. Without consulting others, each individual rates each statement.
4. After all group members have completed their own individual rankings, a group ranking can be sought.

Worksheet 32.1

INTER-RACIAL, INTERCULTURAL, AND INTERNATIONAL VALUES

Indicate your agreement or disagreement with the following statements by circling the appropriate number.

	Strongly agree	Agree	Neutral	Disagree	Strongly Disagree
1. Our country should have the right to prohibit certain racial and religious groups from entering it to live.	5	4	3	2	1
2. Immigrants should not be permitted to come into our country if they compete with our own workers.	5	4	3	2	1
3. It would be a dangerous procedure if every person in the world had equal rights which were guaranteed by an international charter.	5	4	3	2	1
4. All prices for exported food and manufactured goods should be set by an international trade committee.	5	4	3	2	1
5. Our country is probably no better than others.	5	4	3	2	1
6. Race prejudice may be a good thing for us because it keeps many undesirable foreigners from coming into this country.	5	4	3	2	1
7. It would be a mistake for us to encourage certain racial groups to become well educated because they might use their knowledge against us.	5	4	3	2	1

	Strongly agree	Agree	Neutral	Disagree	Strongly Disagree
8. We should be willing to fight for our country without questioning whether it is right or wrong.	5	4	3	2	1
9. Foreigners are particularly obnoxious because of their religious beliefs.	5	4	3	2	1
10. Immigration should be controlled by an international organization rather than by each country on its own.	5	4	3	2	1
11. We ought to have a world government to guarantee the welfare of all nations welfare of all nations irrespective of the rights of any one.	5	4	3	2	1
12. Our country should not cooperate in any international trade agreements which attempt to better world economic conditions at our expense.	5	4	3	2	1
13. It would be better to be a citizen of the world than of any particular country.	5	4	3	2	1
14. Our responsibility to people of other races ought to be as great as our responsibility to people of our own race.	5	4	3	2	1
15. An international committee on education should have full control over what is taught in all countries about history and politics.	5	4	3	2	1
16. Our country should refuse to cooperate in a total disarmament program even if some other nations agreed to it.	5	4	3	2	1
17. It would be dangerous for our country to make international agreements with nations whose religious beliefs are antagonistic to ours.	5	4	3	2	1
18. Any healthy individual, regardless of race or religion, should be allowed to live wherever he wants in the world.	5	4	3	2	1
19. Our country should not participate in any international organization which requires that we give up any of our national rights or freedom of action.	5	4	3	2	1
20. If necessary, we ought to be willing to lower our standard of living to cooperate with other countries in getting an equal standard for every person in the world.					

	Strongly agree	Agree	Neutral	Disagree	Strongly Disagree
21. We should strive for loyalty to our country before we can afford to consider world brotherhood.	5	4	3	2	1
22. Some races seem to be less intelligent than others.	5	4	3	2	1
23. Our schools should teach the history of the whole world rather than of our own country.	5	4	3	2	1
24. An international police force ought to be the only group in the world allowed to have armaments.	5	4	3	2	1
25. It would be dangerous for us to guarantee by international agreement that every person in the world should have complete religious freedom.	5	4	3	2	1
26. Our country should permit the immigration of foreign peoples even if it lowers our standard of living.	5	4	3	2	1
27. All national governments ought to be abolished and replaced by one central world government.	5	4	3	2	1
28. It would not be wise for us to agree that working conditions in all countries should be subject to international control.	5	4	3	2	1
29. Patriotism should be a primary aim of education so our children will believe our country is the best in the world.	5	4	3	2	1
30. It would be a good idea if all the races were to intermarry until there was only one race in the world.	5	4	3	2	1
31. We should teach our children to uphold the welfare of all people everywhere even though it may be against the best interest of our own country.	5	4	3	2	1
32. War should never be justifiable even if it is the only way to protect our national rights and honor.	5	4	3	2	1

Discussion

The statements included in the exercise represent a range of views on values in cross-cultural interaction. There are no necessarily right or wrong answers. As such, it is useful to focus discussion on substance of the statements and their implications. What methods did the group use in its attempts at concensus? Which methods were most effective? How representative of the individual preferences is the overall group ranking? Were some group members more successful at influencing the group than others. (One way to gather information on this question is to ask all participants to add up the differences between their personal scores and the overall group score across all statements. The smaller the "difference score," the closer the individual was to the ultimate group rank.) What kinds of leadership were present in the decision-making process? Democratic? Authoritarian? Was the leadership effective? Did all members participate equally in the decision-making? How well does the final ranking represent individuals in the group? How well did the group tolerate opinions which were not consistent with the majority? Additional dimensions may be usefully underscored through the use of process observation guides.

33. Cross-Cultural Bargaining and Negotiation

The goals of MARKET DAY are to promote simulated intercultural interaction between two groups (here, buyers and sellers), and to develop an understanding of bargaining as a social and economic activity. Each group experiences feelings of being rich or poor, having too much, or having to do without. The simulation may also be utilized to heighten awareness of family decision-making patterns, and develops group solidarity and cultural awareness on the part of nationals from third world countries.

Procedure

1. A working committee of individuals from several third world countries is important for the success of the game. This committee can share information on markets in their own country and help to make decisions for setting up the market simulation. Decisions need to be made about physical space (out-of-doors, with some available shade is desirable), the kinds of foods which can be prepared and sold, and the kinds of character roles to be played. Participation of these nationals is also essential for the replication of selling styles and to demonstrate bargaining tactics. Market characters to be role-played should resemble a motley crowd in a village bazaar, such as beggars, preachers, fortune tellers, magicians, jugglers, hustlers, lottery salesmen, blind musicians, pick-pockets, medicine men, jewelry and clothing peddlers. These characters can be active during the entire market, or appear on the scene for frequent "happenings." For a more realistic market, one might add a few squawking chickens, some assorted garbage, and a fish stall. Those not playing any character-roles can manage stalls (high or low tables, or mats on the ground) typically ornamented with baskets, mats, colored cloth, etc. All nationalities should be encouraged to wear traditional dress for added color. Typical bargaining behavior should be demonstrated along with street cries and shouts of hawkers.
2. Foods can be sold raw or cooked. The following are suggestions for some foods. Most can be found in ethnic grocery stores that cater to such communities.

mangoes	rice	rice cakes
bananas	peanuts	candy
coconuts	cashews	sugar cake
avocadoes	chickpeas	rice and curry
limes	plaintains	akla cakes
plums	fruit juices	cornmeal mush
oranges	ginger beer	soya bread
papaya	moby	plaintain porridge
tunas (prickly pears)	limade	groundnut soup
cassava	fried plaintain	meat pies

3. Start preparation at least one week in advance. Meet with different nationals frequently to develop interest, ideas and methods for conducting of the market simulation activity.
4. Decide on a method of financing the market.
5. Decide which foods will be prepared and which will be sold raw. Buy some foods, such as Jamaican meat pies, from a restaurant if this is possible. Encourage the nationals of various countries to do food shopping for authenticity of such items. If cooking is done, arrange for facilities, utensils, and ingredients.
6. Obtain clothing, lottery tickets, and jewelry if these are easily available. Order paper plates, utensils and cups for serving the food.
7. Provide live traditional music if musicians are available or play taped native music.
8. Decisions about the relative buying power of rich and poor should be predetermined in accordance with the purpose of the market. The "poor" may be at the subsistence farmer level with just enough money to buy only the most coarse and tasteless foods. The "rich" person (urban tourist or foreigner) might have unlimited spending money and be able to buy more frivolously. The affluent, however, must wear an identifying label and take their chances at the bargaining stalls. The middle class are the sellers or business people.
9. Divide the group into approximate percentages with:

    70%   peasants or poor farmers
    20%   rich people
    10%   middle class

10. Envelopes with different amounts of tokens, or chips, or "phony" dollars are made up into individual and family units and sold at $2.00 each before the market opens.
11. The message in the envelope of the "rich" reads:

    Dear Participant,
    For purposes of today's market, you have arbitrarily been chosen to be a member of the richer class. You (and the members of your family) have been given $10.00 worth of chips, which will represent your buying power for the day. You (and members of your family) must wear the enclosed tag, which will identify you to the local community. You are required to spend all your money by the end of the market day, which lasts approximately 2 hours. EAT WELL! ENJOY YOUR WEALTH!

    The "rich" envelope contains $10.00 worth of chips.

    Value of Chips

    Blue—2 chips @ $2.00 each..............$4.00
    Red—3 chips @ $1.00 each..............$3.00
    White—12 chips @ $0.25 each..............$3.00

The message in the "poor" person's envelope reads:

Dear Participant,

For the purposes of today's market, you have arbitrarily been chosen to be a member of the poorer class in your country. You (and your family) have been given $0.85 worth of chips as your total buying power. As a member of the poorer class, you are expected to make this money go as far as possible and to get the best value you can. You are required to spend all your chips by the end of the market day, which lasts approximately two hours. BARGAIN HARD! SHOP WISELY!

The "poor" envelope contains $0.85 worth of chips.

Value of Chips

Green—1 chip @ $0.25 ....$0.25
Orange—4 chips @ $0.10 each............$0.40
Purple— chips @ $0.05 each............$0.20

12. If the market is to be realistic food must be sold at supply and demand prices. In many cases, the "rich" will be able to influence market prices, and keep them inflated, thereby making it almost impossible for the poor to afford those prices. However, the "seller" may vary his prices somewhat, because the poor are much better at bargaining and also represent his main customers on a regular basis. Nevertheless, if a "rich" person approaches the "seller" while the "poor" is pressing for a lower price, the "seller" would inevitably have to sell to the one who can pay the most. Instructions to the seller are: *Vary Prices According to What the Traffic Can Bear!*

The "seller's" envelope contains $1.50 worth of chips in order to make change.

Value of Chips

Green—4 chips @ $0.25 each............$1.00
Orange—3 chips @ $0.10 each............$0.30
Purple—4 chips @ $0.05 each............$0.20

These are the basic prices for the food on sale

Akla Cake-0.15¢
Groundnut Soup-0.20¢ per cup
Rice-0.10¢ per spoonful
Curry-0.05¢ per spoonful
Fried Plaintain-0.15¢
Meat Pies-0.80¢
Avocados-0.60¢ each
Sugar cane-$2.00 for each stalk
Lottery ticket-$1.00 each

Candy (Chinese)-2 for .05¢
Lemonade-0.10¢ a glass
Other drinks-0.10¢ a glass
Oranges-0.10¢ each
Fried Bananas-0.20¢ each
Peanuts-0.10¢ per cup
Cassava-0.05¢ each
Coconuts-0.60¢ each
Mangoes-$1.00 each

Variations

1. The cost of the market, the amount of buying power, the types of items sold, the use or non-use of simulated buying power may be modified according to the goals of the group using this simulation.
2. The role of the family in the simulation may be emphasized or diminished according to the participant population.
3. The activity could be designed primarily as an "eating experience," which would serve to heighten the awareness of different foods, methods of cooking and eating habits.
4. A subsistence meal could be served as a money-raising event, or as an introduction to discussions on world food problems. In this case, everybody would be "poor" and would experience momentary empathy for people living at the poverty level.

Discussion

Participant reactions can be explored around tasting new foods, eating with fingers, dealing with varying prices instead of one fixed price, or the ethics or bargaining. What is a hard bargain and how does one know when one has overstepped cultural norms? What is the value of time in a culture where one has to haggle so long to buy a banana? How does it feel to be rich, particularly when everyone else has so much less? Or, how does the person eating corn meal mush feel about the person enjoying a mango? To what extent did participants "feel" poor? How does this market differ from markets in other countries? What were the group's cultural biases about cleanliness, smells, new foods, time spent in haggling over price, and the social demands of bargaining? How did these influence attitudes and behaviors?

34. Cross-Cultural Development Case Studies

The following case studies are constructed to highlight particular aspects of cross-cultured communication and development. Each of the cases provided in this exercise is intended to stimulate discussion of one or several issues central to cross-cultural adaptation, effectiveness, and development. The primary function of the cases is to point to the tremendous gap that exists in the "knowledge and attitude" of those seeking to relate to their new colleagues in another country and the people who receive them in their new environment.

These case studies may be used with either large or small groups. The objectives may be delineated by either the instructor or a facilitator, whose role is primarily directing questions at the participants. Some of these goals may include seeking explanations from participants of how they arrived at a particular consensus or solution; why they believe it is most appropriate; what alternative solutions they rejected; how certain they are it will work, etc.

These case studies require approximately 30 minutes each to complete.

Procedure

1. Distribute copies of one (or several) of the cross-cultural case studies provided in Worksheets 34.1 through 34.5.
2. Participants may then be grouped, or may work through the cases individually.
3. Ask individuals to read and thoroughly analyze each case study being used.
4. Cases can be discussed with the group as a whole, or participants can be grouped in numbers of 2 to 8, with the assignment of discussing the questions for a case, and deciding upon answers with which the rest of the group members agree.
5. Again, depending upon the numbers of participants involved, and the purposes of the instructor or facilitator, reports from each small group may stimulate further discussion by the other participant groups.

Worksheet 34.1

CROSS-CULTURAL CASE (A)

Mr. S has accepted a consultant position in another country. The project with which Mr. S will be involved is a new one. He will be working directly with Mr. Akwagara, a national; together they will have administrative responsibility for the project.

Mr. S is eager to arrive at his posting. His experience in his own country seems exceptionally well-suited to the task he must accomplish in his country-of-posting, and his high level of motivation and record of consistently superior achievement reassure him that he'll encounter little that he can't handle in his assignment.

After having been on the job for several weeks Mr. S is experiencing considerable frustration. To Mr. S it appears that Akwagara and most of the subordinates lack both training and motivation. On a number of occasions Mr. S has endeavored to point out to Akwagara tactfully, that his practices are both inefficient and ineffective. Akwagara's responses seem to indicate total disinterest. On one occasion, Mr. S suggested that he and Akwagara get together during an evening for a few drinks thinking that in a social setting he might be better able to make Akwagara aware of some of these problems. Nearly every effort to bring up the work situation by Mr. S was followed by Akwagara changing the subject to unrelated chatter about family and friends.

The problem became increasingly severe in the weeks that followed. It seemed to Mr. S that the only way he could get the job done he was sent to do, was to do it mostly himself. Gradually, he assumed more and more of the responsibilities which had previously been performed by Akwagara. Though he feels some concern about this situation from time to time, these feelings are more than compensated for by the knowledge that he is getting the job done which he was sent to do.

Discussion Questions

What has happened?

Should Akwagara be replaced?

How would you assume Akwagara might be feeling about Mr. S? About the project?

Is Mr. S failing or succeeding?

If you were the government aid officer responsible for the project, how would you assess Mr. S's performance thus far? How would you assess the situation in general?

What, if any, are his major problems? What should be done?

Focal Issues—(Case A)

1. Success and achievement in one culture may not well predict success in another culture—particularly where the one culture values speed, efficiency, and effectiveness, and the other does not.
2. Prior to studying a culture one should exercise considerable caution before assuming that he or she is going to have no difficulties in adapting and being successful.
3. Several weeks in a new culture is clearly not a sufficient time period to conclude much of anything—particularly when the culture is one in which the pace of activity is slower than the culture from which one has come.
4. Efficiency and effectiveness are reflective of a particular set of cultural values. Neither is inevitable, nor essential, nor "right."
5. What may look like a lack of "training" and "motivation" from the perspective afforded by one culture, may look like interest, progress, and rapid change from another cultural perspective.
6. What is "idle chatter about family and friends" when considered from one cultural perspective, may be the essence of social interaction, trust, and friendship, from the perspective of another culture where personal and family matters are regarded more seriously than work.
7. Short-term success in terms of "getting the job done," can easily be *failure* in terms of facilitating permanent change and development. "Getting the job done" may be less important than fostering positive interpersonal relationships and effectively transferring skills to individuals with whom one is working.

Worksheet 34.2

CROSS-CULTURAL CASE (B)

John has been going through a period of confusion. He has been less than happy at his job, and opportunities for advancement seem doubtful. With the economy as it is, chances for seeking another position are also less than ideal.

John became aware of an opportunity to be considered for a posting in a country in Western Africa; the government needs someone with his experience. Those aspects of his vocational training which were beginning to become outdated in his country, lessening his chances for promotion, are exactly those that were needed in the development effort. The pay is good, living expenses would be minimal and it's a chance to get away.

Discussion Questions

Should he apply for the posting?

What are the pluses? In the short run? In the long run?

What are the negative factors? In the short run? In the long run?

What are some possible problems he should expect if he applies and is accepted?

What can he do about these problems?

Focal Issues—(Case B)

1. What are appropriate motivations for going to another culture to work?
2. Is there a relationship between one's motivations and the likelihood of happiness, success, adaptation, or effectiveness in a job setting?

Worksheet 34.3

CROSS-CULTURAL CASE (C)

Dr. B together with his wife and two children have accepted a foreign advisory position with the government and are now posted to an outlying village in one of the African countries. Dr. B coordinates a project designed to stimulate the development of a series of community medical stations capable of providing medical assistance to the many residents unable or unwilling to travel to the larger hospitals.

Mrs. B is a registered nurse and has served many years in both volunteer and professional capacities in the health care systems in her own country. She is as eager as her husband to become active in projects to upgrade medical care in the area.

The family has been settled for several weeks and Dr. B has begun initial assessment of the level of medical care in the community. The children are enrolled in a nearby school and all is going smoothly in that respect. Mrs. B decides she will initiate contact with the local hospital and speak to the administrator about her background and qualifications, and offer her services to provide training for nurses and medical assistants.

A meeting is arranged at which time the hospital administrator explains to Mrs. B that in his country it is not customary for women to serve in teaching or supervisory capacities—especially in hospitals. Mrs. B said she understood, and explained that no doubt that custom had developed simply because there had been no women available with the necessary training and experience to teach or supervise. She explained further that she was certain she could serve the interests of the community and upgrade the level of skill and knowledge of nurses and medical assistants if permitted to supervise training courses. Reluctantly, the administrator consented. After several months of volunteer work in supervising training sessions, Mrs. B began to experience severe frustration and periods of depression. Attendance at the training sessions had been scanty to begin with, and had dropped off steadily to the point where only one or two persons from the hospital staff showed up for training. Her presence in the hospital, even when not in the training sessions, was met by indifference by the members of the hospital staff. Her relations with her husband, Dr. B were also quite strained in this environment.

Dr. B was himself experiencing a great deal more frustration in gaining the momentum he had expected toward progress in establishing the medical stations. His every step was thwarted and his plans stymied by bureaucratic red tape, and eventually hopes for the expansion of satellite medical units seemed out of the question. In fact he considered prospects for significant improvement in the situation to be exactly zero. To make matters worse, family relations were tense, and Mrs. B was especially alienated on account of her sad experience in her professional encounters.

Discussion Questions:

In general, what went wrong?

What could Dr. B have done to avoid some of these problems?

What could Mrs. B have done?

What should Dr. B do now?

What should Mrs. B do?

Focal Issues—(Case C)

1. The expectations associated with the male and female role may differ dramatically from one culture to another.
2. Customs and traditions develop over a long period of time within a culture. Even when the demands or exigencies of a situation change, customs may change very slowly or not at all.
3. In some cultures (on occasion within our own), "consent" does not always imply agreement with the substance of another person's ideas or proposals. It may simply imply deference to the other's higher status, or be indicative of a less aggressive communication style.
4. Violation of cultural customs or traditions may preclude contributing one's knowledge and/or skills.
5. Negative or positive communication outcomes are often unrelated to one's intentions.
6. The dissatisfaction of one member of a family, can become a source of stress and dissatisfaction for the family as a whole.
7. In cultures with more "traditional" concepts of the female and wife role, a woman's behavior—in this case the violation of custom and tradition—may become perceptually linked and "spill-over" to the perceptions people have of her husband.

Worksheet 34.4

CROSS-CULTURAL CASE (D)

The Q family has been in Meditania for nearly 60 days. Prior to departure all members of the family were very enthusiastic at the prospect of travel and the chance to contribute to world progress and development. Travel had always been one of the interest which the members of the Q family had in common.

Mr. Q accepted a position as coordinator of an important aspect of a new project. Mr. Q has been prominent within his field in his own country, and enjoys the respect and admiration of his colleagues. Mr. Q is an avid hockey fan, and at home wouldn't miss the Sunday pro football games on TV, if he could at all help it. The Qs' enjoyed socializing on weekends with associates from work and friends from the neighborhood.

Before moving, Mrs. Q had become very active in social and service club organizations, and eagerly anticipated the opportunity to continue her interests in their new country.

Prior to their move, Mary, 17, had greatly enjoyed her past two years in school, and had achieved a fine scholastic record. She had taken an active role in school athletics and was a member of the cheerleaders. She was elected Vice-President of her class and enjoyed an active social life.

Discussion Questions

What problems might Mr. Q encounter in adapting his life style to his new home?

What problems might Mrs. Q be confronted with?

What are some possible difficulties Mary may encounter?

Are there some difficulties which might confront the family as a whole?

To what extent are these difficulties totally unique to the Qs?

What are some strategies or considerations which might ease some of Mr. Q's difficulties? Mrs. Q's? Mary's? The family's?

Focal Issues—(Case D)

1. Travel to a different culture may have little in common with living there for a period of time. In the former case, no permanent adjustment is required. In the latter, it is.
2. The life styles of one culture are seldom duplicated in another culture.
3. Social success in one culture may not necessarily transfer to social success in another culture.
4. Adjustment to differing lifestyles and social circumstances can lead to some unhappiness and frustration, at least in the short run.

Worksheet 34.5

CROSS-CULTURAL CASE (E)

Ms. Blank volunteers her services, upon graduation, to serve with a village uplift project in a developing country. Her responsibilities are to organize and promote literacy clubs for rural area girls.

She is assigned to a supervisor, Mr. X, who is also a Westerner. He has been reasonably successful at organizing boys' clubs throughout the country as a part of a large agricultural extension project. He had no knowledge of the decision to involve Ms. Blank in a project with the village girls, and he seems a bit put-off by his exclusion in her selection and briefing.

In planning her approach to the project, Ms. Blank followed the system which she was accustomed to in her own country. This pattern meant that Ms. Blank went directly to the girls, organizing her clubs through schools. This was exactly opposite to the approach used by Mr. X; he began by seeking the participation of parents. As is customary in Western countries, Ms. Blank opened her meetings with singing by the girls. She advised the girls at one of the earlier meetings that their goal was to encourage development and modernization in their homes and in the village. She introduced the girls to Western clothing practices and encouraged them to try to adopt them in their everyday wear.

Responses to the first meetings of the girls' clubs varied. The girls were extremely enthusiastic. The fathers, however, objected to the clubs because they believed their daughters were becoming harder to manage. The religious leaders of the village stated that they considered singing at the club meetings to be sacrilegious. The mothers expressed some concern about the assertiveness of their daughters. However, the daughters themselves responded very positively to Ms. Blank's instructions. As a result of this mixed reaction to the situation, Ms. Blank was summoned by her supervisor for consultation.

Discussion Questions:

What are some of the things the supervisor is likely to point out to Ms. Blank?

Is Ms. Blank failing or succeeding?

Should the program be terminated?

Should it be changed?

Should Ms. Blank be encouraged to remain in the position she is in now?

What can be done for obtaining a satisfactory solution to such problems?

Focal Issues—(Case E)

1. The approaches that are successful in one culture, may not be so in another culture.
2. In any culture, there is much to be gained from thoroughly studying approaches which have succeeded, before embarking on a new plan.
3. Development efforts will be impeded by not taking into account the traditions and customs of the culture in which one is operating.
4. In developmental efforts, it is often necessary to balance one's concerns for rapid, short-run change, with an awareness of the desirability of slower, long-run progress.

Discussion

Each of the cases provided in this exercise is intended to stimulate discussion of one or several communication issues central to cross-cultural adaptation, effectiveness, and development. The cases are based on real incidents, modified for instructional purposes. Clearly, there are no single right or wrong answers for any case. Especially with the limited amount of information provided with each, it is impossible to arrive at *the* solution to any of the problems involved. The primary function of the cases, then, is to improve participant awareness of the sorts of problems involved in cross-cultural communication and to broaden the range of alternative problem-definitions and the solution-strategies available.

As a guide to the sorts of theoretical issues which may be persued with cross-cultural case studies, summaries of *Focal Issues* are provided for each case.

35. Language and Cross-Cultural Communication

This game highlights some of the dynamics involved in cross-cultural interaction utilizing a language which is not shared by both parties. Additionally, it underscores the role of non-verbal dimensions in cross-cultural communication. The activity can be used with any number of pairs of individuals, and requires approximately one hour to conduct.

Procedure

1. Pair off participants, asking that members of each dyad sit facing one another, at some distance from other dyads.
2. Provide one member of each dyad with a *Lobu Language Guide* (provided in Worksheet 35.1) and the second member of each dyad with an *Aku Language Guide* (provided in Worksheet 35.2).
3. Instruct participants that they are not to show their language guides to their dyad partners.
4. Distribute copies of Worksheet 35.3, one per participant which provides the *Rules for the Game*.
5. Distribute Worksheet 35.4 (*Lobu Language Tasks*) to the member of each dyad who previously received the *Lobu Language Guide* (Worksheet 35.1).

    The *Lobu Language Tasks Worksheet* details several simple tasks which the Lobu-speaking dyad member is to try to get his or her partner—who does not speak Lobu—to perform. Only Lobu may be used—*No English*. As the rules indicate, he or she may couple Lobu words with non-verbal actions, indicating the referents for the words, pointing to his or her own nose and saying ''Dolp,'' for example.
6. The Lobu-speaking dyad partner proceeds to explain in Lobu each of the ten tasks indicated on the *Lobu Language Tasks Worksheet* (35.4), one at a time. Following each, the speaker records his or her assessment of how well his or her partner was able to complete the task, by circling either ''failure,'' or ''success.'' On the *Lobu Language Tasks Worksheet*.
7. When all ten tasks have been completed, the other member of each dyad—the Abu-speaking individual—is provided with a copy of the *Abu Language Tasks Worksheet* (35.5). Abu-speakers are to go through their ten tasks, one at a time, using no English. They rate their successes at communicating with their Lobu-speaking partner for each task by circling ''failure,'' or ''success,'' on the *Abu Language Tasks Worksheet*.

Worksheet 35.1

LOBU LANGUAGE GUIDE

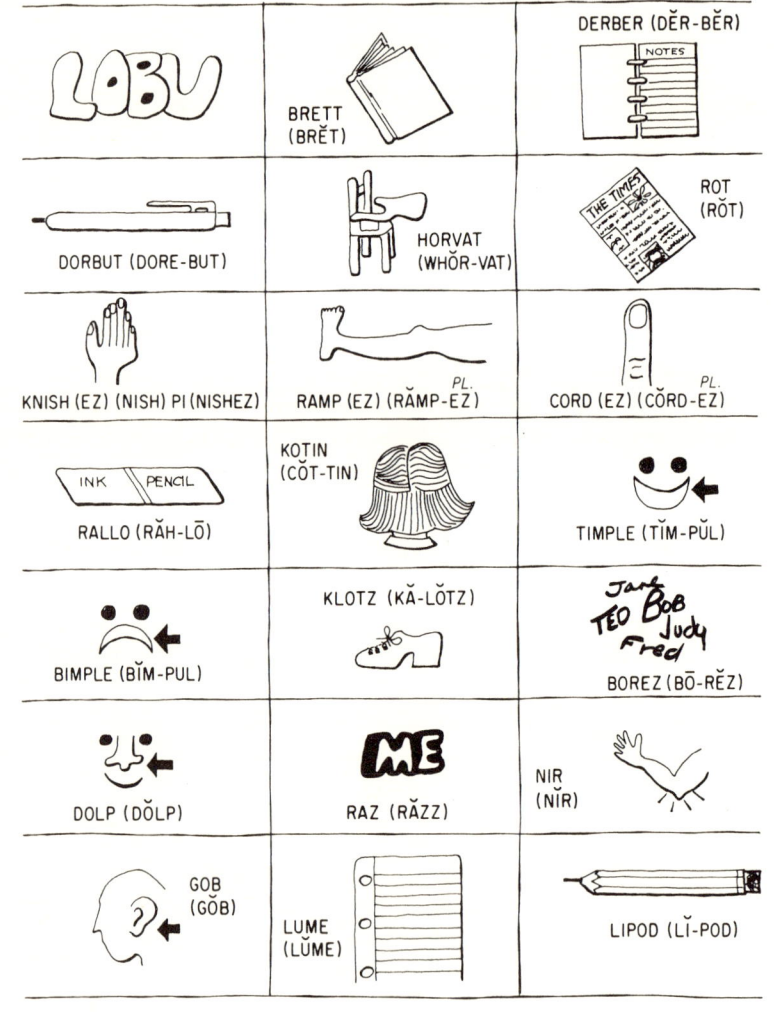

Worksheet 35.2

ABU LANGUAGE GUIDE

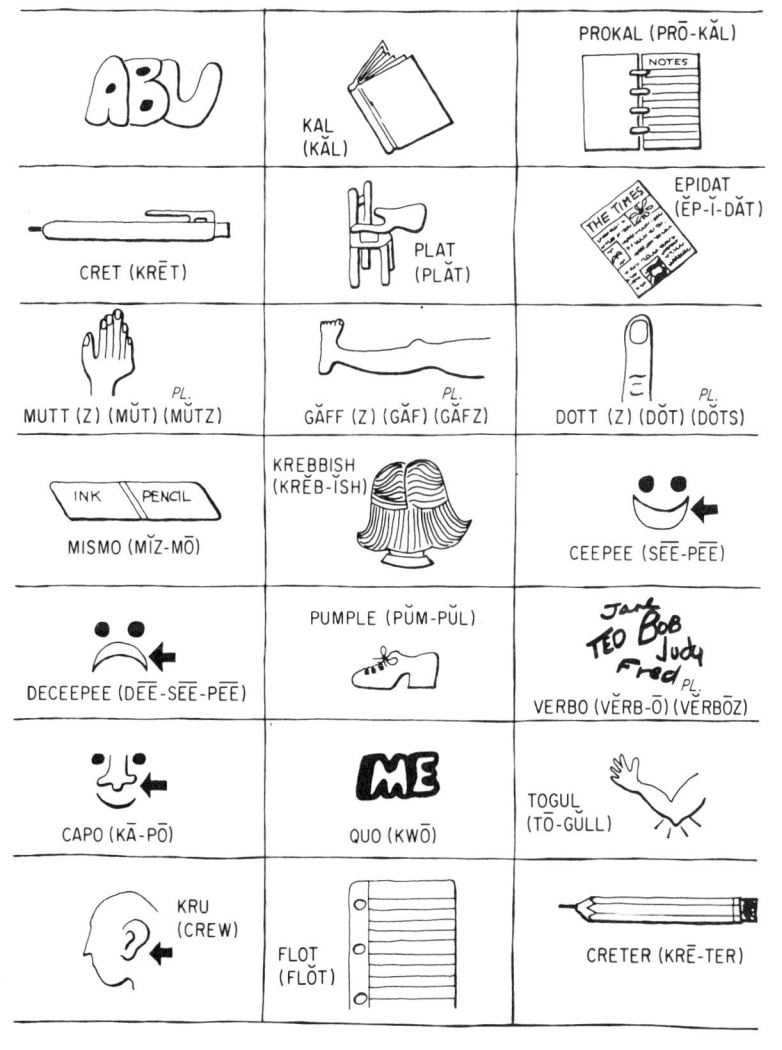

Cross-Cultural and Intercultural Communication

Worksheet 35.3

RULES

READ CAREFULLY BEFORE YOU BEGIN. NO QUESTIONS MAY BE ASKED.

1. KEEP YOUR SHEET TO YOURSELF. *DO NOT* SHARE IT WITH YOUR PARTNER.
2. NO LANGUAGE OTHER THAN THE SIMULATED LANGUAGE MAY BE USED AT ANY TIME.
3. ON YOUR FIRST ATTEMPT TO COMMUNICATE, YOU ARE ONLY PERMITTED TO USE THE WORDS FOR THE OBJECTS ON THE SHEET WITH *NO* CONSCIOUS NON-VERBAL COMMUNICATION OR ACTION.
IF YOUR PARTNER DOES NOT UNDERSTAND WHAT YOU WANT, THEN, AND ONLY THEN MAY YOU REFER TO YOUR NON-VERBAL REPETOIRE. NON-VERBAL SYMBOLS AND SIGNS CAN BE GIVEN, HOWEVER, YOU *MAY NOT DIRECTLY POINT TO OR TOUCH THE OBJECTS BELONGING TO YOUR PARTNER THAT ARE INVOLVED IN THE TASK.*
4. YOU MAY NOT PERFORM THE ACTION, BUT YOU MAY INDICATE.
5. THE SIMULATED LANGUAGE WORD FOR EACH OBJECT *MUST BE SPOKEN EACH TIME* AN INDICATION ABOUT THAT OBJECT IS MADE.

Worksheet 35.4

LOBU LANGUAGE TASKS

GET YOUR PARTNER TO:

1. Put his elbow on the desk.
2. Give you a pencil.
3. Cross their legs.
4. Take off a shoe.
5. Frown.
6. Tear a piece of paper in half.
7. Say their name.
8. Stick a pencil behind their ear.
9. Put a pen on top of a notebook.
10. Cross a pen on top of a pencil on the desk.

INDICATION OF HOW SUCCESSFULLY TASK WAS COMPLETED. (CIRCLE ONE.)

1. Failure/Success
2. Failure/Success
3. Failure/Success
4. Failure/Success
5. Failure/Success
6. Failure/Success
7. Failure/Success
8. Failure/Success
9. Failure/Success
10. Failure/Success

Worksheet 35.5

ABU LANGUAGE TASKS

GET YOUR PARTNER TO:

1. Put elbow on notebook.
2. Smile.
3. Roll pen up in a piece of paper.
4. Cover their nose with their hand.
5. Fold their hands.
6. Fold a piece of paper.
7. Give you a pen.
8. Put their hair on the desk.
9. Take off a shoe.
10. Cross their legs.

INDICATION OF HOW SUCCESSFULLY TASK WAS COMPLETED. (CIRCLE ONE.)

1. Failure/Success
2. Failure/Success
3. Failure/Success
4. Failure/Success
5. Failure/Success
6. Failure/Success
7. Failure/Success
8. Failure/Success
9. Failure/Success
10. Failure/Success

Discussion

While the game provides only a highly artificial simulation of interpersonal interaction with someone who uses a different language, it can be a viable means for raising awareness of some of the basic issues involved. It is useful, for example, to consider the basic cognitive and affective responses one has when confronted with a situation that demands familiarity with a language with which one is not familiar. Further, the basic processes by which a second language is learned—or may be learned—is suggested by the pairing of vocabulary words with non-verbal indications of the object to which a given word refers. In this context, the importance of gestures, body movements, facial expressions, and illustration, for coping with and comprehending concepts in another language, can be explored from data generated by this exercise.

It also can be noted that both languages are composed only of nouns, with no verbs to reference actions. Was this noticed by participants? What role if any did it play in attempts at instruction-giving and comprehension?

As appropriate, the instructor may wish to explore the relationship between language structure and reality perception in this context. If one's language stressed object names, and categories—as English does, for example—would one learn to see a different reality, than if one's primary language were stressed verbs, processes, and dynamics—as some Eastern languages do? Do the labels one has for his or her experiences influence what one can see?

What were some strategies that facilitated successful completion of the tasks? Which factors impeded success? To what extent was the game experience realistic? In which respects was it realistic? In what respects unrealistic?

PART 4

MASS COMMUNICATION

Mass communication is a one-to-many message selection and sending process. It occurs when symbolic realities that are created through social communication are diffused to large numbers of diverse individuals, who ingest and use them for relating to their environment and one another.

Through social communication, relationships are defined. As noted earlier, dyads, families, groups, organizations, and societies are all created, maintained, altered and/or changed through social communication processes. When such relationships or systems involve more than a few persons—and when those persons are separated in space or time—message-sending networks are essential in order to maintain relationships among the components of the system—the people. It is mass communication which facilitates the preservation, ordering, transmission, and integration of social system symbols across space, through time, and among diverse individuals, thereby providing the basis for shared symbols and continuity of relationship.

At a less abstract level is the mass communicator. Essentially, the mass communicator is an individual who serves as an agent to his or her mass audience, by selecting, abstracting, interpreting, and re-directing the messages available in the environment. In so doing, the mass communicator provides a second order environment for audience members to use as a basis for behaving relative to one another, the Social system, and their environment. In the process, the currency necessary for continued social exchange is also generated.

In this perspective the mass communicator is viewed as a mediator between the individual members of his or her audience and their environment. The role is an active, rather than passive one.

The agent—the mass communicator— is subject to all the dynamics of personal and social communication. There is no value-free way to select or interpret information from the environment. Similarly, there is no single, correct approach to message selection or interpretation. Thus, the obligation of the mass communicator to be sensitive to the dynamics of personal communication is critical. Because, mass communicators seldom function in a social vacuum, and are themselves operating and simultaneously being influenced by a number of personal, social, and professional relationships, the nature of social communication is also important to understanding the manner in which mass communicators function in both theory and practice.

Quite clearly, the manner in which the professional mass communicator selects, arranges, diffuses his or her interpretations of the important messages in the environment, has implications not only for the mass communicator, but for members of their audience as well. Whether the messages in question are informational, entertaining, or promotional in nature, the dynamics of the process are essentially the same.

The activities included in this section of the volume are intended to supplement exercises dealing with personal and social communication, and to highlight those dimensions of human communication of particular relevance to the mass communicator or journalist. Accordingly, exercises are included which focus on interviewing and perception, information acquisition, written communication, levels of analysis, context, message design, style, and information selection and display.

Bibliography

Budd, Richard W. and Brent D. Ruben, *Mass Communication,* Rochelle Park, N.J.: Hayden, 1977.

McLuhan, Marshall, *Understanding Media,* New York: Signet, 1964.

Ruben, Brent D. and John Y. Kim (Eds.), *General Systems Theory and Human Communication,* Rochelle Park, N.J.: Hayden, 1975.

Westley, Bruce H. and Malcolm S. MacLean, Jr., "A Conceptual Model for Communication Research," *Journalism Quarterly,* Vol. 34, 1975, pp. 3-38.

36. Biographical Interviewing

This exercise provides an opportunity for participants to practice fundamentals of biographical interviewing, biographical writing and evaluation. It can be used with 3-100 participants and requires approximately 60 minutes to complete.

Procedure
1. Participants are asked to develop what each believes to be ten questions that should be asked of another individual to provide the basis for a reasonably thorough biographical sketch.
2. Participants are grouped in triads (groups of 3 persons each).
3. Proceeding in order, each participant interviews the other two individuals in his or her group, asking the ten questions previously developed.
4. Using the resulting interview data, each participant writes a biographical sketch of the two persons he or she interviewed.
5. Completed biographical sketches are submitted to interviewees who rank the two in order of their adequacy, providing a statement of rationale with each.

Discussion
What kinds of questions were selected? How were they selected? Were they appropriate? What values and assumptions were reflected in the questions? Were they oriented to the needs of the interviewer, the interviewee or both? Could they have been improved? How were the questions received? What problems were encountered in writing the biographical sketches? How were the two interviews evaluated? What factors contributed to having a bio-sketch accepted? How adequately did bio-sketches match the interviewee's image of themselves? How can discrepancies be explained? What aspects of this exercise are especially relevant to interviewing for mass media?

37. Interviewing and Perception

This exercise focuses on fundamental dynamics of interviewing, and the role of perception in information gathering. It can be used with any number of persons, and requires approximately one hour to complete.

Procedure

1. Instruct participants that they are to select a building and conduct an interview with it.
2. Following their interviewing of the building, participants are asked to write a brief summary of the building (one to two pages) without ever mentioning the building by name.
3. Participants are grouped into triads (groups of threes).
4. The building-interview stories are exchanged within triads, and the two other members of the triad read the stories and try to determine the identity of the building based upon them.

Discussion

Are there fundamental differences between interviewing a building and interviewing a person? What are those differences? Are there similarities? What are they? What sorts of interview questions proved useful for the assignment? What sorts of information was it important to acquire? What kinds of information led to the identification of the buildings by other triad members? What sorts of information inhibited building-identification? What interviewing skills and insights can be drawn from the building-interviews that have relevance for interviewing people? What writing and perceptual skills that came into play in the exercise, have relevance for mass communication in general?

38. Written Communication

This exercise deals with the preparation and evaluation of technical, scientific and instructional writing. It can be used with 10 or 50 participants and requires from 1-3 hours to conduct.

Procedure

1. The facilitator purchases several sets of any of a variety of goods requiring assembly. Examples are childrens toys, dress patterns, hobby kits, tinker toy or erector set models, or household items such as shelving units, log-bins, grass-catchers, bicycle carriers, etc.
2. One item is assembled and used as a display model.
3. One unassembled kit—less instructions—is provided to each of the 3-6 participant groups (to a maximum of five groups).
4. Each group is charged with the task of developing precise, assembly instructions which provide the necessary information to complete the kit in the same manner as the display. (An example is provided in Fig. 38.1.)
5. Participants are encouraged to develop "Instructions" which are brief, precise, and to-the-point, since their "Assembly Instructions" will be tested.
6. When completed, each group's "Instructions" are collected and distributed randomly, one each, to groups of uninitiated participants, who will compete to complete their kits working from the instructions provided. The display model is placed out of sight so that the group's written "Assembly Instructions" are the only source of information for correct construction of the kits.
7. The facilitator records the time necessary for each group to complete the kits.
8. Following completion of the items, assembly group members are asked to review their operation, focusing on the instructions, and dealing with its strengths, weaknesses, ambiguities, errors, etc.
9. The group which prepared the instructions may listen to and/or participate in the discussion of their respective "Assembly Instructions."

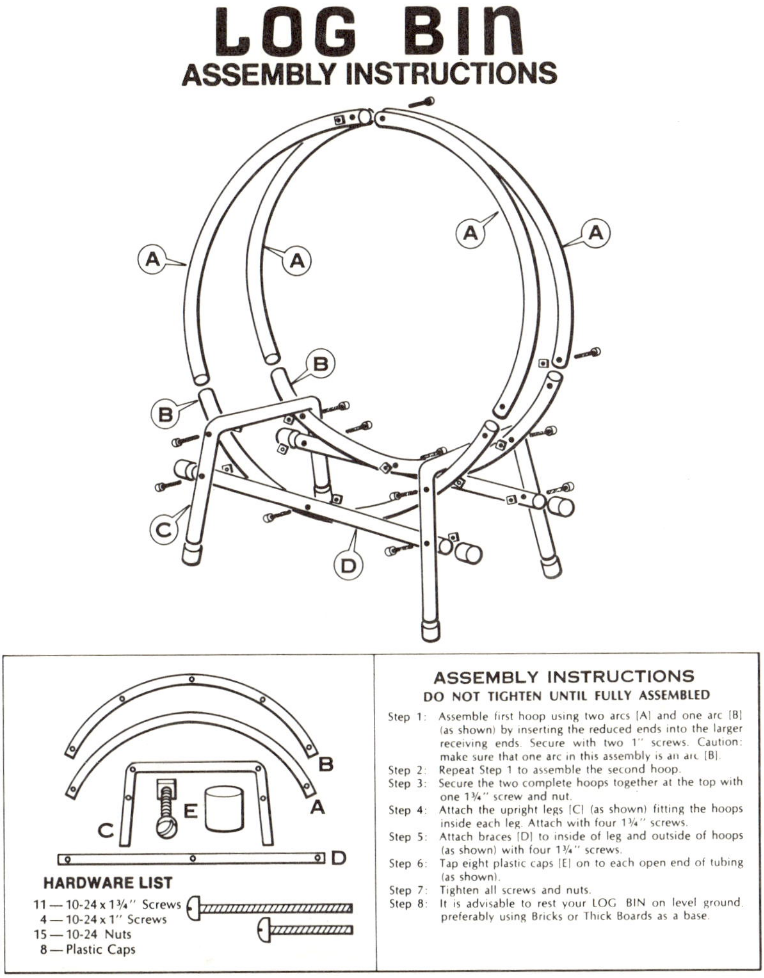

LOG BIN
ASSEMBLY INSTRUCTIONS

ASSEMBLY INSTRUCTIONS
DO NOT TIGHTEN UNTIL FULLY ASSEMBLED

Step 1: Assemble first hoop using two arcs [A] and one arc [B] (as shown) by inserting the reduced ends into the larger receiving ends. Secure with two 1" screws. Caution: make sure that one arc in this assembly is an arc [B].
Step 2: Repeat Step 1 to assemble the second hoop.
Step 3: Secure the two complete hoops together at the top with one 1¾" screw and nut.
Step 4: Attach the upright legs [C] (as shown) fitting the hoops inside each leg. Attach with four 1¾" screws.
Step 5: Attach braces [D] to inside of leg and outside of hoops (as shown) with four 1¾" screws.
Step 6: Tap eight plastic caps [E] on to each open end of tubing (as shown).
Step 7: Tighten all screws and nuts.
Step 8: It is advisable to rest your LOG BIN on level ground, preferably using Bricks or Thick Boards as a base.

HARDWARE LIST
- 11 — 10-24 x 1¾" Screws
- 4 — 10-24 x 1" Screws
- 15 — 10-24 Nuts
- 8 — Plastic Caps

Fig. 38.1

Discussion

How were various "Assembly Instructions" alike? How did they differ? Which seemed most effective? Which required the least time to follow? Which were the shortest? Which used illustrations? What formats and factors seemed to generally facilitate effective written instructional communication?

39. Perception, Levels of Analysis, Context

This exercise is designed to increase awareness of the role of level of analysis and context upon journalists' perceptions. The activity can be used with any number of participants, and requires approximately 45 minutes to conduct.

Procedure

1. Display the picture provided in Figure 39.1 (or an equivalent).
2. Ask participants to write a one paragraph description of the situation characterized in the picture.
3. Display a second picture—the one provided in Figure 39.2 (or its equivalent), and again ask participants to write a one paragraph description of the situation portrayed.

Fig. 39.1

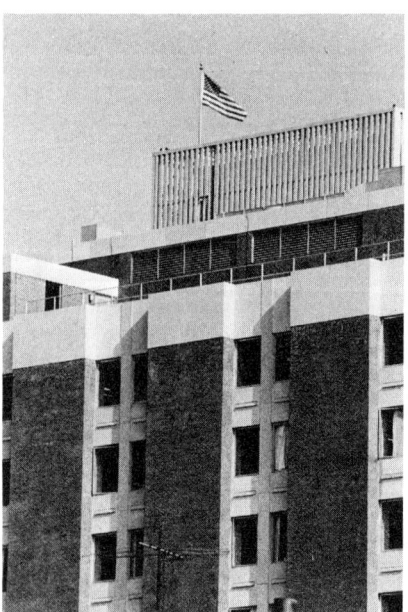

Fig. 39.2

4. Display Figure 39.3, and then 39.4, in turn, with instructions after each to write descriptive paragraphs.

Fig. 39.3   Fig. 39.4

Discussion

Are all four pictures of the same situation? Why? Why not? Aren't all four pictures of the flag? What, then, are the differences between the flag as characterized in the picture provided in Figure 39.1 compared to the flag as portrayed subsequently. These questions provide the basis for a useful discussion of the concepts of level of analysis and context, and an exploration of the extent to which one's view of a situation or event may be dramatically affected by the chosen level of analysis and the amount of contextual information provided. In some senses, a change in level of analysis, perspective, or context of an event or situation, leads to a significant change in one's view of the event itself. How do the concepts of level of analysis relate to the mass communicator or journalist? To the photographer? To perception in general? What implications can be drawn from this exercise that have pertinence to the journalist or mass communicator?

40. Message Design and Style

This exercise provides a simple message design and rewrite problem. It can be useful for discussing variations in writing style, and the relationship of style to audience, context, and intended function. The activity can be used with any number of participants, and requires approximately 30 minutes to complete.

Procedure

1. Distribute copies of the restaurant place mat provided in Fig. 40.1, to each participant.
2. Ask that participants rewrite the narrative on the place mat in a style they think would improve upon the rough copy. Indicate to participants that in addition to grammatical correctness and clarity, they should strive to convey an inspiring image of Mayberry's Restaurant and Marina.
3. Optionally, participants can be asked to design the art portions of the place mat as well as the narrative.
4. Group participants in clusters of 4 persons, have rewrites exchanged, and are allowed 15 minutes for reading and comment.

Discussion

There are, of course, a number of ways the narrative material could be revised to improve upon the rough-draft version, depending upon one's sense of the best image to provide for the restaurant, and particular stylistic preferences. The conceptual thinking which preceded rewrites, stylistic choices, and outcomes can be a point of departure for discussion. Several examples of rewrites are provided in Worksheets 40.1–40.4, and may be used for discussion and comparison.

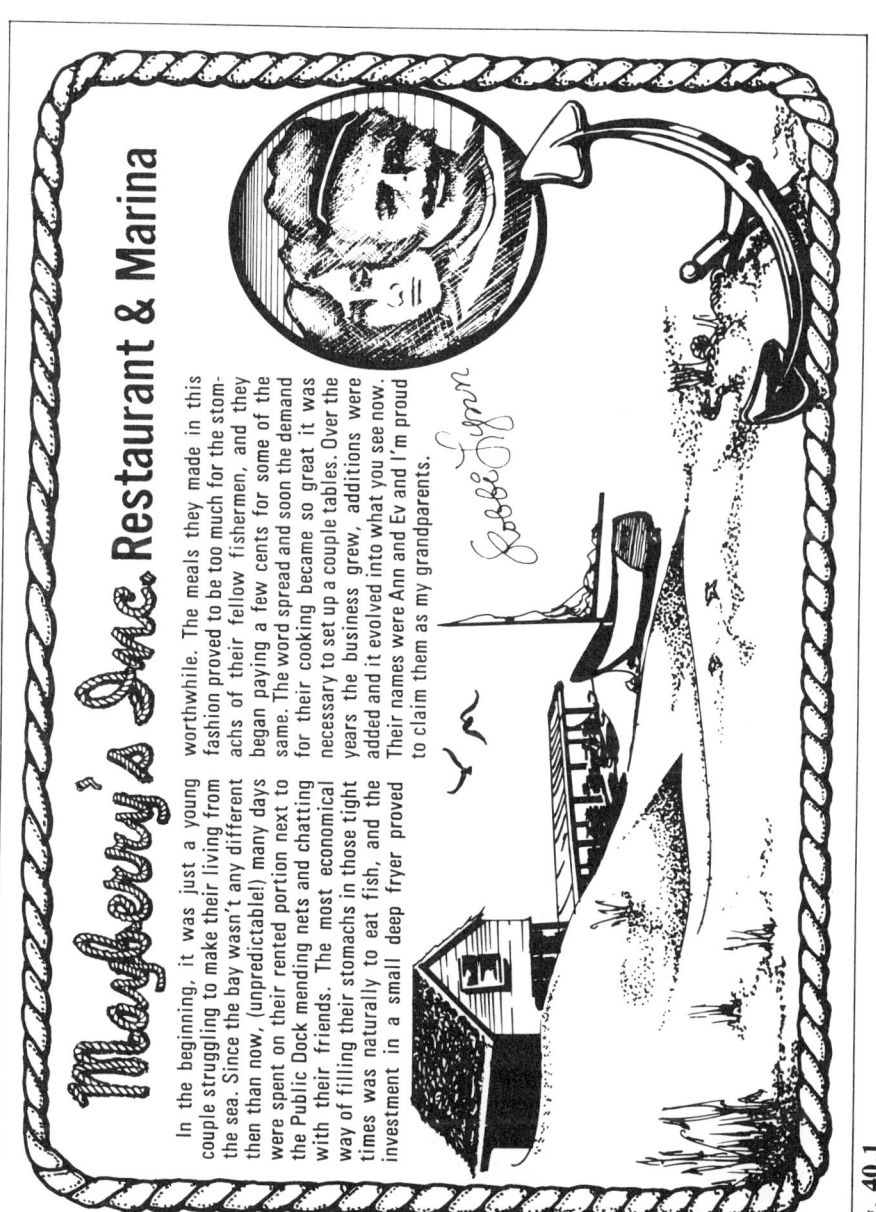

Fig. 40.1

Mass Communication

Worksheet 40.1

REWRITE NO. 1

I'm proud to claim Ann and Ev Mayberry as my grandparents. They started out as a young couple struggling to make their living from the sea. Since the sea was as unpredictable then as it is now, they spent many days on their rented portion of the dock, mending nets and chatting with their friends.

The most economical way to fill their stomachs was fish, and the investment in a small deep-fryer proved worthwhile. The meals they made in this fashion much impressed their friends and fellow fishermen, who began paying a few cents for the deep-fried delights. The word spread and soon the demand for their cooking became so great it was necessary to set up a couple of tables.

Over the years, the business grew and it evolved into what you see now. The tradition of fine seafood like Ann and Ev's, continues here at Mayberry's.

Worksheet 40.2

REWRITE NO. 2

Ann and Ev Mayberry were a young couple struggling to make a living from the sea; a precarious existence, since a good catch was never guaranteed. Many days were spent near the public dock, mending nets and chatting with friends.

Times were hard, and the cheapest thing to eat was fish. The small deep-fryer purchased by the Mayberrys helped prepare many an enjoyable meal for their fellow fishermen, who were soon willing to pay for the pleasure. The word spread, and it became necessary to set up a couple of tables to meet the demand.

Mayberry's Inc. Restaurant and Marina is a result of years of growth and improvement. The place where you now sit would probably be a barren dock were it not for the efforts of Ann and Ev Mayberry. I am proud to call them my grandparents.

Worksheet 40.3

REWRITE NO. 3

While you're waiting for your meal, I thought you might enjoy the story of how our family's restaurant began.

My grandparents, Ann and Ev Mayberry, loved the sea. They spent many days at this bay, on the dock mending nets and chatting with friends while waiting for the fish to bite.

Fish were not only exciting to catch, but also provided a nutritious and economical meal for the newly married couple. Investing in a deep-fryer gave them the opportunity to try new methods of preparing the fish, which they often shared with their friends at the dock.

Enthusiasm for the food served at Mayberrys' spread rapidly, and the young couple began a small business which prospered. Today it is much bigger, and I am proud to be the manager of the restaurant forged from such humble beginnings.

Worksheet 40.4

REWRITE NO. 4

The story of Mayberry's is a true fish tale. When Ann and Ev first rented their portion of the public dock, they found that the cheapest way to live was to eat what they caught. Because of the unpredictability of the sea, Ann soon learned new ways to dress up and stretch their meals.

Ann's reputation as a cook soon spread to fellow fishermen and they began to pay a few cents to sample her good cooking. The demand became so great that soon Ann and Ev had to set up tables to handle the increasing numbers of people.

Over the years the business grew until they opened a restaurant. It evolved into what you see now, and also, we hope, has never lost the personal touch Ann and Ev Mayberry gave it in those early days, long ago.

41. Information Selection and Display

This exercise focuses on aspects of the editing and gatekeeping process. It underscores the active nature of gatekeeping functions, and the relationship of message selection to audience preference patterns. The activity requires approximately two to three hours and can be used with any number of participants larger than 12.

Procedure

1. Participants are formed into groups of 3 to 5 persons in either a random or purposeful manner, depending upon the instructor's goals.
2. Each group is given an identical collection of wire copy stories or a collection of fabricated news and feature items.
3. Distribute a copy of Worksheet 41.1 to each group which provides basic Instructions for the exercise.

Worksheet 41.1

INFORMATION SELECTION AND DISPLAY

Instructions:

SPECIFICATIONS: pages 8½ × 11 mimeo, stapled at upper left or stapled at side margins.

Titles: ½-inch and/or ¼-inch heads set all caps, or typewriter face all caps and underline.

Columns: 9⅛" deep by 3⅜" (or 7") wide.

WORK TO BE PERFORMED BY EACH TEAM:

1. Select articles from packet for use.
2. Indicate on layout forms how the articles are to be displayed. You may cut articles to any length. If you cut by more than 10%, note in margins why sections have been omitted. Stories may be combined as desired.
3. Allow adequate space for headlines, including white "buffer" space. Actual headlines may be written if you desire.
4. Design and schedule on the layout form a nameplate for the first page of the newsletter.
5. Photographs cannot be included. Write a memo to the publisher suggesting art or graphics (line drawings only).
6. Submit a memo explaining which three articles have been given the greatest emphasis (most space; best "play") and justify your editorial judgment.

Worksheet 41.2
DUMMY SHEET

4. Also distribute to each group a number of "dummy" pages (provided in Worksheet 41.2). The number of pages provided should be appropriate to the amount of wire copy or other materials they will be selecting from. (Depending upon the goals of the instructor, groups may be asked to edit materials by as much as 70–75% if emphasis is to be placed on news criteria and editing practices. If the primary function of the exercise is layout and packaging, it may not be necessary to ask that more than 15–25% of the original material be edited out.)
5. Each group prepares copies of its completed informational packet and distributes one to each of the other groups.
6. Each group evaluates all of the other group's packets and provides narrative feedback to each group, as well.
7. The assessments are provided to the respective groups as one evaluative measure of their work.
8. It may be useful, depending upon the nature of the material being edited and the instructor's goals, to have packets also evaluated by other audiences, such as instructor(s), media professionals, individuals characteristic of the average audience member, i.e., average newspaper reader, etc.

Discussion

Which group packets were ranked highest? Why? Which packets were ranked lowest? Why? Were all packets rated similarly by all audience members? If there were major differences, of what were these assessments reflective? To what extent did news values and perceptions of the audience, influence information selection and display considerations by the groups?

The dynamics within groups may also be explored. What sorts of leadership patterns developed. Were all group members in agreement as to the approach that should be taken to information selection and packaging? How were disagreements handled? Did the majority view prove to be the best?

PART 5

COMMUNICATION OBSERVATION AND RECORDING GUIDES

Beyond actual participation in experience-based learning activities, a great deal can be learned about the dynamics of human communication by observing, describing, and analyzing social interaction from a semi-detached perspective. The guides in this section are designed to facilitate this kind of learning. Each form focuses its user's attention on particular elements of the communication process, and will provide an important adjunct to the exercises, games, and simulations.

While the activity of observing and recording communication behavior is sometimes perceived by participants as less exciting than direct involvement in the simulations and games, the value of the role, both for the observer and the observed, clearly warrants its utilization. Rotating participants through both active participatory roles as well as the more detached observer and reporter function provides a maximally impactful and integrative learning experience. It is particularly desirable for observer reports to be fed into post-exercise discussions. In this manner, the observer feedback provides an additional point of view than the individuals who participated directly, and their reactions to the feedback will serve to help sharpen the observational and descriptive skills of the observer.

Observers will find it useful to distinguish between the *content of communication* and the *process of communication*. Content refers to what is being talked about—the subject of discussion. It is, of course, the dimension with which participants will be most familiar. Topical outlines, who says what to whom and in what order, storyline and plot have been experiences common to most students.

The process of communication is likely to be a much less familiar, far more subtle, and difficult to grasp concept for observers. It deals not with what is discussed, but rather *how* it is discussed. Process analysis focuses on the dynamics of leadership, levels of participation, modes of decision-making, patterns of influence, modes of verbal and nonverbal contribution, and so on.

One particularly useful approach to process observation is the "group-on-group" design. This consists of one group of individuals who participate directly in a decision-making or problem-solving activity, and an outer group of participants—ideally of an equal number who observe the operating group's activity. The *Group Communication Observation Form* is well suited for this situation. After the activity group has completed its task, the observers lead a discussion of the processes of interaction they noted, using the descriptions and observations as the initial impetus.

A variation of this pattern is to have each individual in the task group observed by one, preselected individual from the observation group. The Behavioral Observation Guides are useful for this design. Following the decision-making or problem-solving activity by the work group, the observer and the person he or she observed are paired for a five minute feedback and discussion session. The observer describes the communication behaviors of the person observed. As a part of the discussion, the observed individual may also share his own perceptions of his behaviors, which in some instances may differ markedly from those noted by his observer. In such instances, the more specific the description the observer can provide of the communication behavior of the individual observed, the more likely the information is to be useful to its receiver. *Guidelines for Providing Useful Feedback* suggests additional guidelines.

Observers should be cautioned that in all cases their role is to describe communication behavior, not to judge or evaluate it as "good" or "bad," nor to attempt to explain why certain behaviors occurred. Following paired discussions, it is often useful to reunite the two original groups—workers and observers—to briefly discuss the group processes that were noted. This provides observers the opportunity to share their more general observations with the entire group, and often facilitates discussion of leadership, effects of leadership, group climate, directionality of information flow, and so on. If time permits, the instructor may wish to repeat the exercise reversing the roles of the groups.

Where conditions permit, video taping of many of the exercises in this volume will prove a powerful and valuable expansion of the process observation concept. Where replay of the tape is accompanied by discussion, participants have the opportunity to gain a quite different perspective on their own communication behavior.

Bibliography

Benne, Kenneth and P. Sheats, "Functional Roles of Group Members," *Journal of Social Research,* Vol. 4, No. 2, 1948.

Carkhuff, Robert R., *Helping and Human Relations: Volume I,* New York: Holt, Rinehart and Winston, 1969.

Carkhuff, Robert R., *Helping and Human Relations: Volume II,* New York: Holt, Rinehart and Winston, 1969.

Hanson, Philip G., "What to Look for in Groups: An Observation Guide," in J. W. Pfeiffer and J. E. Jones (Eds.), *The 1972 Annual Handbook for Group Facilitators,* La Jolla, Calif.: University Associates Press, 1972.

Miel, Alice, "A Group Studies Itself to Improve Itself," *Teachers College Record,* Vol. 49, No. 1, October, 1947, pp. 31–43.

National Training Laboratories, "Feedback and the Helping Relationship," *Reading Book,* 1967.

Ruben, Brent D., "Assessing Communication Competency for Intercultural Adaptation," *Group and Organization Studies,* Vol. 1, No. 3, 1976, pp. 334–354.

Wiemann, John M., "An Experimental Investigation of Communication Competence in Initial Interactions," New Brunswick, N.J.: Institute for Communication Studies, 1976.

1. Descriptions of Common Roles in Interpersonal and Group Communication

The following description of common roles in groups can be used as a basis for observing behavior in interpersonal and small group communication situations. Typically no one individual serves only in a single role, rather he or she may move in and out of several of these roles within a short period of time. These categories should therefore be looked upon as descriptions of particular modes of behavior, rather than of people.

A. Task Oriented Roles:

Facilitation and coordination of group problem solving activities.
1. Initiator:
   Offers new ideas or changed ways of regarding group problems or goals. Suggests solutions. How to handle group difficulty. New procedure for group. New organization for group.
2. Information seeker:
   Seeks clarification of suggestions in terms of factual adequacy and/or authoritative information and pertinent facts.
3. Information giver:
   Offers facts or generalizations which are "authoritative" or relates own experience pertinently to group problem.
4. Coordinator:
   Clarifies relationships among ideas and suggestions, pulls ideas and suggestions together, or tries to coordinate activities of members of sub-groups.
5. Evaluator:
   Subjects accomplishment of group to "standards" of group functioning. May evaluate or question "practicability," "logic," "facts," or "procedure" of a suggestion or of some unit of group discussion.

B. Relation Oriented Roles:

Building group-centered attitudes and orientation.
6. Encourager:
   Praises, agrees with, and accepts others' ideas. Indicates warmth and solidarity in his attitude toward members.
7. Harmonizer:
   Mediates intra-group scraps. Relieves tensions.
8. Gatekeeper:
   Encourages and facilitates participation of others. "Let's hear . . ." "Why not limit length of contributions so all can react to problem?"

9. Standard setter:
   Expresses standards for group to attempt to achieve in its functioning or applies standards in evaluating the quality of group processes. Raises questions of group goals and purpose and assesses group movement in light of those objectives.
10. Follower:
    Goes along somewhat passively. Provides friendly audience.
11. Group-observer:
    Stays out of group's proceedings; functions by giving feedback as to what goes on during various phases of the meeting.

C. Self-Oriented Roles:

Tries to meet felt individual needs often at the expense of group.

12. Blocker:
    Negativistic. Stubbornly and unreasoningly resistant. Tries to bring back issue group intentionally rejected or by-passed.
13. Recognition-seeker:
    Tries to call attention to himself. May boast, report on personal achievements, and in unusual ways, struggles to prevent being placed in "inferior" position, etc.
14. Dominator:
    Tries to assert authority in manipulating group or some individuals in group. May be flattery, assertion of superior status or right to attention, giving directions authoritatively, interrupting contributions of others, etc.
15. Avoider:
    Maintains distance from others. Passive resister. Tries to remain insulated from interaction.

2. Role Behavior Recording Form

Study the role descriptions provided in the following form. Then for each group member place a check in the column corresponding to the role most often filled by each.

Roles

Group Members

Role	A	B	C	D	E	F	G	H	I	J	K	L	M	N
1. Initiator Contributor														
2. Information Seeker														
3. Information Giver														
4. Coordinator														
5. Evaluator														
6. Encourager														
7. Harmonizer														
8. Gatekeeper														
9. Standard Setter														
10. Follower														
11. Group Observer														
12. Blocker														
13. Recognition Seeker														
14. Dominator														
15. Avoider														

3. Group Communication Observation Form

This form provides a basic framework for observing, recording and studying some elements of the communication dynamics which operate in small group interaction.

Interpersonal Communication

1. Expressing (verbal and non-verbal)
2. Listening
3. Responding

Communication Pattern

1. Directionality (one-to-one, one-to-group, all through a leader)
2. Content (thoughts, feelings, etc.)
3. Influence (who talks to whom, who looks at whom for support?)

Major Roles*

_____ Initiator	_____ Gatekeeper
_____ Information Seeker	_____ Standard Setter
_____ Information Giver	_____ Follower
_____ Coordinator	_____ Observer
_____ Evaluator	_____ Blocker
_____ Encourager	_____ Recognition Seeker
_____ Harmonizer	_____ Dominator

*Role descriptions provided in Role Behavior Recording Form.

Leadership Style

1. Was the main leadership pattern democratic?
2. Was the main leadership pattern dictatorial?
3. Did a "do your own thing" leadership style prevail?

Effects of Leadership

1. Was participation generally good?
2. Was there a lack of enthusiasm by participants?
3. Did commitment seem low?
4. Were some participants holding back?

Participation

1. Who were the most active participators? Which participants were not active?
2. Were there major shifts in levels of participation during the activity?
3. How were low participators treated? How was their silence interpreted?

Influence

1. Who were the most influential members in the group? Who were the least influential?
2. Were there major shifts in sources of influence during the activity?
3. How many suggestions were rejected?

Decision-Making

1. How were decisions made? By voting? Consensus? Ramrodding?
2. How focused was the group on its main topic of concern?
3. Were there particular clusters of group participants who would usually support one another in arriving at decisions? Were there groups or individuals who were frequently in conflict with one another?
4. How involved were all group members in arriving at decisions?
5. How did the group resolve major differences of opinions?

Norms

1. Were there certain topics which were generally avoided by the group (for example, religion, race, feelings for one another, sex, points of disagreement, etc.)?
2. Did members of the group conduct themselves in particularly polite or formal ways? Were members conducting themselves in a manner that seemed especially informal?
3. Were individual's feelings dealt with openly?
4. Were individual's motives dealt with openly?

Goals

1. Were group goals discussed?
2. Were the goals agreed upon?
3. Did the group accommodate diverse goals?

Cohesion

1. Did group members tend to perceive situations similarly?
2. Did membership in the group provide interpersonal rewards?

Group Climate

1. How would you characterize the general climate of the group?
2. Do members get together socially, outside of formal group sessions?
3. Did members of the group seem to have sincere regard for one another's thoughts and feelings?

Situational Factors

1. What were the effects of the group size?
2. Was time a factor in the group's process?
3. Were physical facilities an important factor in determining the nature of interaction (for example, seating arrangement, tables, etc.)?
4. Were all members present for entire interaction?

4. Recording Information Networks

Observing message flows within a group can be useful for studying and reporting upon such factors of group communication as influence, status, interpersonal attraction, participation, attention, etc.

Procedure:
1. Record the order of speakers, either directly as the meeting progresses or from tape recordings afterward.
2. Pictorially depict message flow pattern as follows:
    a) draw a circle using group members' names or initials as points along its circumference as in Fig. 4.1.

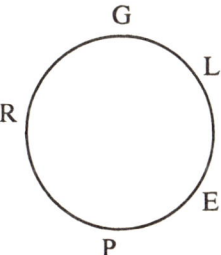

Fig. 4.1

b) Indicate message initiation by drawing lines from the first speaker to the next to the next and so on; where overlapping occurs, curve lines slightly so they will be apparent. (i.e. Record—Ron, Gayle, Ron, Pat, Ed, Lynn, Ron... as in Fig. 4.2.

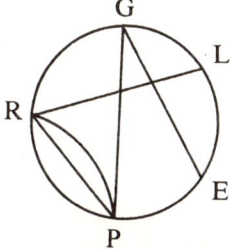

Fig. 4.2

5. Small Group Interaction Content Guide

In group meetings, especially those of a task-oriented nature, it is, of course, desirable for a major portion of the discussions to remain on the subject at hand. Group members are often unaware of straying from the topic. This guide suggests a means of studying and reporting on a group's topical patterns.

Instructions:
1. Using audio or video tape recorder, record a group discussion.
2. Transcribe individual's statements onto paper.
3. Categorize each statement, starting with the first as either on the subject or off the subject. (For these purposes "on the subject" can be defined in one of two ways: 1) using the first statement of the session as the establishment of the subject, or 2) using the first statement that directs the group's attention to the task or task-related matter as the subject topic.)
4. Develop a table, entering group members' names vertically and the two categories: "on-the-topic" and "off-the-topic" horizontally as in Fig. 5.1. Note: where desirable the table may be presented without indicating the names of individuals.

	on-topic	off-topic
Ed	𝍱 (5)	//
Gayle	/	
Pete	𝍱 𝍱 (10)	

Fig. 5.1

5. Place a tally-mark for each section of conversation in the section corresponding to the names of the speaker as shown in Fig. 5.1. When complete the result will provide a useful individual and group profile.

6. Intra-Group Perception Guide

The following method of observation involves direct questioning of group members in order to visually display some of the underlying patterns or relationships operating within a group. Patterns can be developed to explore a variety of dimensions, such as "who feels closest to whom within the group", "who do you consider to be the leader in the group," or "who looks to whom for negative feedback," etc.

Procedure:

1. Select the basis upon which a sociogram is to be constructed and develop a question or questions to get at the matters of concern.
2. At a session where *all* members can be asked the same questions at the same time, read off questions asking each member to respond in writing indicating one other group member's name. (i.e. Who do you feel closest to?—Ron)
3. After questions and answers are completed collect answer-sheets from each participant, making sure he or she has put his or her name on the paper as well.
4. To construct the sociogram, use one piece of paper for each question. Arrange members' names in circular order on the page, as in Fig. 6.1.

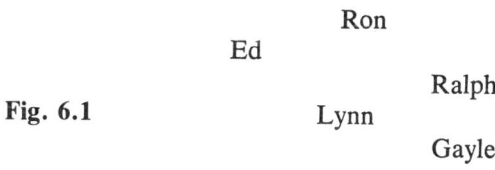

Fig. 6.1

5. Record answers by drawing lines from name of person answering to the person indicated as in Fig. 6.2.

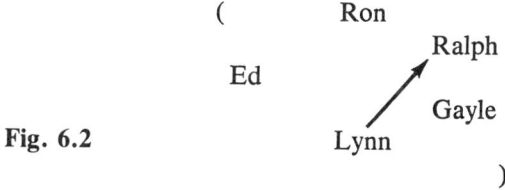

Fig. 6.2

Follow this procedure until all members have an arrow from their name to the person indicated. Continue until all questions have been displayed in this manner.

6. Clearly, any number of patterns may appear, for example if no one indicates a particular person for an answer, that person can be diagrammatically depicted as an isolate as in Fig. 6.3.

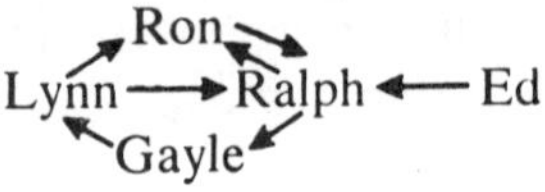

```
        Ron
      ↗    ↘
Lynn ──→ Ralph ←── Ed
      ↖    ↙
       Gayle
```

Fig. 6.3   (Here Ed might be considered an isolate.)

If one person is chosen by an overwhelming majority of responses, that can be diagrammatically depicted as a star structure as in Fig. 6.4.

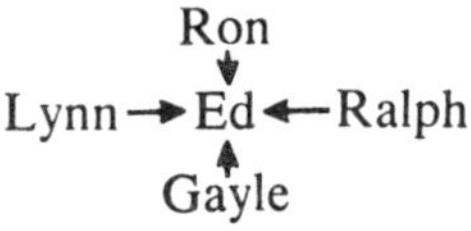

```
           Ron
            ↓
    Lynn → Ed ← Ralph
            ↑
          Gayle
```
Fig. 6.4

Often in larger groups subgroups may be in evidence. They can be depicted as a triangle as in Fig. 6.5.

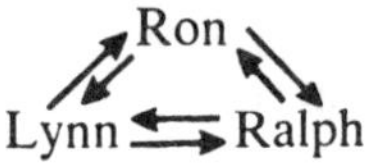

```
         Ron
        ↗  ↘
      ↙      ↘
   Lynn ⇌ Ralph
```
Fig. 6.5

7. Verbal Interaction Recording Guide

This method of process observation involves recording the duration of verbal interaction and silences. It is useful in observing and recording patterns of participation and sequences of conversation flow.

Procedure:
1. Develop a table entering group members' names vertically and time sequences in units of 15 seconds each, horizontally.
2. Either by recording directly during meeting or by transcribing from tape recorder after the meeting, measure how long a person speaks and place a horizontal jagged line corresponding to the amount of time used, on the line that corresponds to the speaker.

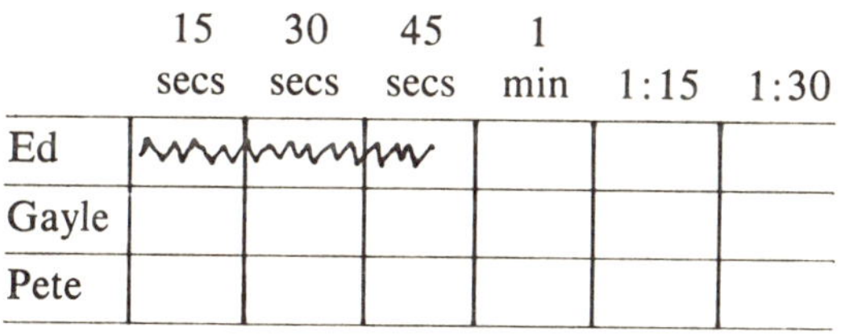

	15 secs	30 secs	45 secs	1 min	1:15	1:30
Ed	∿∿∿∿∿∿∿∿					
Gayle						
Pete						

Fig. 7.1

Fig. 7.1 would indicate that Ed spoke for approximately 40 seconds.

3. To indicate that someone else continued the conversation immediately after the previous speaker stopped, draw a straight vertical line from the jagged line of the last speaker's name to the succeeding speaker at the same time unit on the table as in Fig. 7.2.

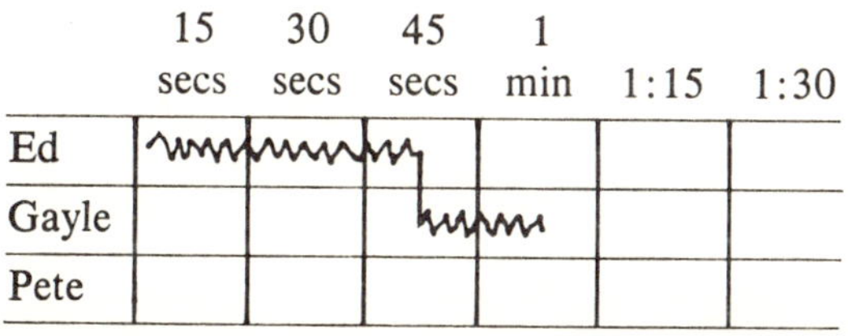

	15 secs	30 secs	45 secs	1 min	1:15	1:30
Ed	∿∿∿∿∿∿∿∿					
Gayle			∿∿∿∿			
Pete						

Fig. 7.2

Fig. 7.2 indicates Gayle has continued the conversation without a break occurring between the two speakers.

4. To indicate that there was a silence between speakers, a slanted straight line from the jagged line of the last speaker is drawn to the following speaker's area indicating the time spent in silence, as shown in Fig. 7.3

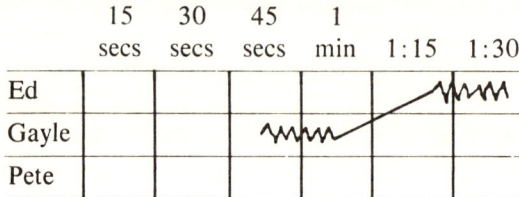

Fig. 7.3

This slanted line indicates a silent period of 15 seconds before Ed spoke after **Gayle**.

8. Seating Arrangement Recording Guide

Seating arrangements are often important to group development. Information about spatial geography can be an aid in distinguishing working conditions such as competition and co-operation, and can be used for inferring patterns of acquaintance, support, leadership, etc.

Procedure:
1. Keep a running record of where group members choose to sit by placing x's and group members' names in corresponding locations on paper as shown in Fig. 8.1.

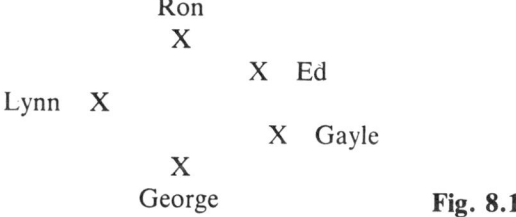

Fig. 8.1

2. If physical barriers are present, place them in the diagram as well as in Fig. 8.2.

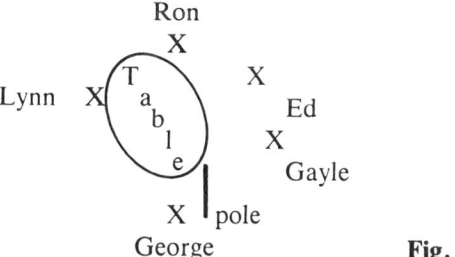

Fig. 8.2

3. If possible, take notes on type of meeting, noting any corresponding changes in discussion and seating arrangements. (Three major patterns emerging in group message networks can be identified: The chain depicting two-way interactions between all members except for the people at the extreme ends.

$$G \leftrightarrow R \leftrightarrow P \leftrightarrow L \leftrightarrow E \qquad \text{Fig. 8.3}$$

The circle (Fig. 8.4) depicting a situation where every member speaks to two other members.

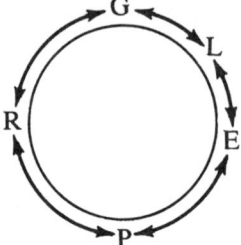

Fig. 8.4

The wheel (Fig. 8.5) depicting one person to which all statements are directed.

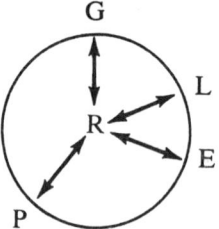

Fig. 8.5

9. Interpersonal Communication Observation Form

This form provides a basic framework for observing, recording, and reporting upon aspects of interpersonal communication. It is by no means a complete listing of the elements of interaction, and serves only as a summary of some observable elements of interpersonal dynamics.

Interpersonal Communication

1. Clarity of expression of thoughts and feelings.
   (a) Verbal
   (b) Non-verbal
2. Range of expression of thoughts and feelings.
   (a) Verbal
   (b) Non-verbal
3. Listens to the thoughts and feelings of others.

General Orientation Categories

1. Task Orientations—Places primary emphasis on completing the task. Shows relatively less concern for the needs, feelings, and concerns of persons involved.
2. Intrapersonal Orientation—Places primary emphasis on his or her own needs, feelings and concerns. Shows relatively less concern for the completion of the task itself or for the other persons.
3. Interpersonal Orientation—Places primary emphasis on the needs, feelings, and concerns of members other than himself. Shows relatively less concern for the completion of the task itself or for his own needs, feelings, and concerns.

Roles in which the person observed functioned (where possible give examples).

*Role descriptions provided in Role Behavior Recording Form.

10. Guidelines for Providing Useful Feedback

Feedback is communication to a person (or a group) which tells how he or she affects others. It can serve as a basis for the individual to correct his communication strategies to enhance the likelihood that the outcomes of his communicating will match his intentions.

Some criteria for useful feedback:

1. It is *descriptive* rather than *evaluative*. By describing one's own reaction, it leaves the individual free to use it or not to use it as he or she sees fit. By avoiding evaluative language, it reduces the need for the individual to respond defensively.
2. It is *specific* rather than *general*. To be told that one is "dominating" will probably not be as useful as to be told that "just now when we were deciding the issue, you did not appear to listen to what others said and I felt forced to accept your arguments or face attack from you."
3. It takes into account the needs of both the receiver and giver of feedback. Feedback can be destructive when it serves only our own needs and fails to consider the needs of the person on the receiving end.
4. It is directed toward behavior which the receiver can do something about. Frustration is only increased when a person is reminded of some shortcoming over which he has no control.
5. It is *solicited*, rather than *imposed*. Feedback is most useful when the receiver himself has formulated the kind of question which those observing him can answer.
6. It is well-timed. In general, feedback is most useful at the earliest opportunity after the given behavior (depending, of course, on the person's readiness to hear it, validation available from others, etc.).
7. It is checked to insure clarity. One way of doing this is to have the receiver try to rephrase the feedback he or she has received to see if it corresponds to what the sender had in mind.
8. When possible, check accuracy of the feedback with others in the group. Is this only one person's impression or an impression shared by others?

11. Individual and Group Climate Guide

The purpose of this exercise is to foster an examination of individual and group mood and changes in mood during group proceedings. The exercise is designed for use with small groups and requires 30 minutes to several hours.

Procedure:
1. Before the activity, prepare 40–50 oak tag or cardboard signs with yarn or string to hang around participants' necks, lettered with the words "I FEEL" and one word describing a particular feeling. A sample of such descriptive words follows:

confident	ambitious	silly
humorous	dynamic	humorless
unhappy	sensitive	accepted
extroverted	scared	mean
open	bored	isolated
quiet	detached	bizarre
motivated	cooperative	friendly
unfriendly	happy	useful
withdrawn	misunderstood	pushy
nervous	rejected	talkative
uncooperative	closed	insensitive
romantic	tense	helpful
observant	ecstatic	introverted
hungry	insecure	tired
frustrated	distracted	obnoxious

2. Arrange signs in a visible location.
3. Have participants think about how they feel at that moment and ask them to choose a sign that represents that feeling and hang it around their neck.
4. Have group proceed in its normal discussions.
5. Remind participants that as the discussion proceeds, their feelings might change and to, therefore, change feeling tags.

Discussion:

What reactions did participants have to the signs? How did the signs affect the group process? Were the signs helpful in your recognition of emotions? Why or why not? How? Did the signs have an effect on members' participation rates? What is the relevance of this exercise for everyday communication situations?

12. Empathy

Participant: _____

Rater: _____

Date: _____

Instructions:

Individuals differ in their skill in projecting an image which suggests they understand things from another person's point-of-view. Some individuals seem to communicate a fairly complete awareness of another person's thoughts, feelings, and experiences, while others seem unable to display any awareness of another's thoughts, feelings, or state-of-affairs. For each individual indicate on a 1 to 5 continuum which pattern of behavior was most characteristic during your observations.

Description

1. *Low Level Empathy:* The individual indicates little or no awareness of even the most obvious, surface feelings and thoughts of others. The individual appears to be bored or disinterested, or simply operating from a pre-conceived frame of reference which totally excludes that of the other persons around at a particular point in time.
2. *Medium-Low Empathy:* The individual may display some awareness of obvious feelings and thoughts of others. The individual may attempt to respond based on this awareness, and often the responses seem only superficially matched to the thoughts and feelings of others involved in the interaction.
3. *Medium Empathy:* The individual predictably responds to others with reasonably accurate understandings of the surface feelings of others around, but may not respond to, or may misinterpret less obvious feelings and thoughts.
4. *Medium-High Empathy:* The individual displays an understanding of responses of others at a deeper-than-surface level, and thus enables others involved in interaction to express thoughts or feelings they may have been unwilling or unable to discuss around less empathic persons.
5. *High Empathy:* The individual appears to respond with great accuracy to apparent and less apparent expressions of feeling and thought by others. Projects interest, and provides verbal and non-verbal cues that he or she understands the state-of-affairs of others.

Rating Scale

1   2   3   4   5

(Place "x" to indicate position on continuum)

13. Orientation to Knowledge

Participant: _____

Rater: _____

Date: _____

Instructions:

Different people explain themselves and the world around them in different terms. Some personalize their explanations, knowledge, and understandings, prefacing their statements with phrases like "*I* feel...", "*I* think..." etc., and might say something like "I don't like Mexican food." Others tend to generalize their explanations, understandings, and feelings, using statements like "it's a fact that...", "It's human nature to...", etc. This pattern of explanation would more likely lead an individual to say "Mexican food *is* very disagreeable..." indicating that the food is the basis of the problem rather than the person's own tastes. For each individual indicate on a 1 to 4 continuum the pattern of expression which was most characteristic during the period of observation.

Description

1. *Intrapersonal Orientation:* Treats perceptions, knowledge, feelings, and insights as personally based, as with a statement such as "I don't like Mexican food" which makes clear that the mismatch between the food and the taster is a consequence of the taster's particular tastes, perceptions, likes, etc., and may have nothing necessarily to do with Mexican food, per se. Differences in perception between people are not problematical. Examples of phrases which may be characteristic of this orientation are, "I feel that...", "It is my view that...", "I believe...", etc.
2. *Interpersonal Orientation:* Treats perceptions, knowledge, and feelings as personal but potentially generalizable to others also. Tends to assume that others in an immediate group will share the individual's perceptions, feelings, or thoughts (as with friends, colleagues, family, other members of a group). An individual whose orientation to knowledge is of this sort might say "No one in my family would like these Tacos." May use phrases such as "we feel...", "My husband and I believe...", "Most of you in the group know that...", "People in my profession...", etc.
3. *Cultural Orientation:* Treats perceptions, knowledge, feelings, and insights as highly generalizable from one individual to another within a culture. Assumes that other persons of similar cultural heritage will almost always share the individual's perceptions, as with a statement such as "North Americans find Mexican food far to hot for their tastes..." May use phrases such as, "in my country...", "Canadians are generally...", "Africans are a highly intelligent people...", "In this culture...", etc.
4. *Physical Orientation:* Treats perceptions, knowledge, feelings, and insights as inherent in the people and objects being perceived. Assumes other people will always share the individual's perceptions, attitudes, and feelings if they are mature, knowledgeable, or insightful. Given this, differences with others' perceptions imply that the other persons' are "wrong" or lack maturity or knowledge. Such an orientation might lead to a statement such as "Mexican food is too hot." The individual of this orientation might use phrases such as "We've all experienced...", "It's human nature...", "That's inevitable...", "What else could they have done...", etc.

Rating Scale

1   2   3   4

(Place "x" to indicate position on continuum)

14. Role Behavior

Participant: _____

Rater: _____

Date: _____

Instructions:

Indicate how often participants exhibited each pattern of role behavior during the time periods observed.

DESCRIPTION

Task Roles:

Individuals differ in the extent to which they engage in behavior that contributes to group problem-solving activities. Activities associated with the completion of task include initiation of ideas, requesting further information or facts, seeking of clarification of group tasks, clarification of task related issues, evaluation of suggestions of others, focusing group on task. Indicate with an "x" how often participants displayed task behaviors.

1	2	3	4	5
never	seldom	occasionally	frequently	continually

Relational Roles:

Individuals differ in the extent to which they devote effort to building or maintaining relationships within a group. Group development activities, as they are sometimes termed, may consist of verbal and non-verbal displays which provide a supportive climate for the group members and help to solidify the group's feelings of participation. Behaviors which lead to these outcomes include harmonizing and mediating scraps and/or conflicts between group members, attempts to regulate evenness of contributions of group members, comments offered relative to the groups dynamics, indications of a willingness to compromise own position for the sake of group concensus, and displays of interest (nods of agreement, eye contact, general attending behaviors), etc. Indicate with an "x" frequency of displayed relational behavior.

1	2	3	4	5
never	seldom	occasionally	frequently	continually

Individualistic Roles:

Some individuals operate in groups in a fashion which tends to be highly individualistic, and as a consequence may serve to block the groups efforts at both problem solving and relationship building. Behaviors of this sort include high resistance to ideas of others; return to issues and points of view previously discussed and acted upon or dismissed by the group; attempts to call attention to him or herself; attempts to project a highly positive image by noting achievements, qualifications, vocational or professional experience or other factors which are designed to increase the individual's credibility; attempts to manipulate group by asserting authority through flattery, sarcasm, interrupting, etc.; actively avoiding and resisting participation, remaining insulated from group when individual feels he or she is not getting their way, etc. Indicate with an "x" the frequency the individual displayed individualistic behavior.

1	2	3	4	5
never	seldom	occasionally	frequently	continually

15. Interaction Management

Participant: _____

Rater: _____

Date: _____

Instructions:

People vary in their skill at "managing" interactions in which they take part. Particularly with regard to *taking turns in discussion* and *initiating and terminating interaction based upon the needs of others,* some individuals display great skill and others less so. For each participant indicate on the 1 to 5 continuum which pattern was most characteristic during your observations.

Description

1. *Low Management:* Individual is unconcerned with taking turns in discussion. May either dominate or refuse to interact at all; unresponsive to or unaware of other's needs for involvement and time-sharing. Initiates and terminates discussion without regard for the wishes of other individuals. May continue to talk long after obvious displays of disinterest and boredom by others involved, or may terminate discussion—or generally withold information—when there is clear interest expressed by others for further exchange.
2. *Moderately Low Management:* Individual is minimally concerned with taking turns in discussion. Often either dominates or is reluctant to interact; often unresponsive to other's needs for involvement and time-sharing. Initiates and terminates with minimal regard for the wishes of other individuals. Conversations are initiated and/or terminated with minimal regard for other individuals.
3. *Moderate Management:* Individual is somewhat concerned with taking turns in discussion. May tend to dominate or provide low interaction profile from time to time, person to person or topic to topic; some concern for time-sharing and initiating and terminating interactions in a manner that is consistent with the needs of others.
4. *Moderately High Management:* Individual is quite concerned with taking turns in discussion. Seldom either dominates or is reluctant to interact with most persons at most times; shows a concern for time-sharing, and initiating and terminating interaction in a manner that is consistent with the needs of other participants.
5. *High Management:* Individual is extremely concerned with providing equal opportunity for all participants to share in discussion. The initiation and termination of discussion always indicates concern for the interests, tolerances, and orientation of others who are party to interaction.

Rating Scale

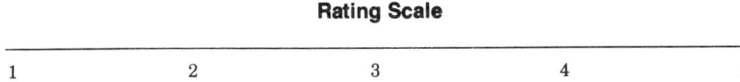

1   2   3   4   5

(Place "x" to indicate position on continuum)

16. Interaction Posture

Participant: _____

Rater: _____

Date: _____

Instructions:

Responses to another person or persons in an interpersonal or group situation range from *descriptive, non-valuing* to *highly judgmental.* Indicate on a 1 to 4 continuum which interaction pattern was most characteristic during observation.

Description

1. *High Evaluative:* The individual appears to respond to others' verbal and non-verbal contributions in a highly judgmental and evaluative manner. The individual appears to measure the contributions of others in terms of a highly structured, predetermined framework of thoughts, beliefs, attitudes, and values. Responses therefore communicate clearly whether the individual believes others to be "right" or "wrong." Reactions are often made in declarative, often dogmatic fashion, and will closely follow the comments of others, indicating little or no effort to digest what has been said before judging it.
2. *Evaluative:* The individual responds to others verbally and non-verbally in an evaluative and judgmental manner; measures the responses and comments of others in terms of a predetermined framework of thoughts, beliefs, attitudes, and values. The framework is not totally rigid, but does provide a clear basis for determining whether others' contributions are "right" or "wrong." Reactions to others tends to follow fairly close on the heels of termination of discussion by other interactants, but there is some break indicating a minimal attempt to digest and consider others' ideas before responding positively or negatively.
3. *Evaluative-Descriptive:* The individual appears to measure the responses of others in terms of a framework based partly on information, thoughts, attitudes, and feelings gathered from the particular interaction and the individuals involved. Offers evaluative responses, but they appear to be less than rigidly held, and subject to negotiation and modification. Time lapse between others' comments and the individual's response suggest an effort to digest and consider input before reacting either positively or negatively.
4. *Descriptive:* The individual responds to others in a manner that draws out information, thoughts, and feelings; provides evaluative responses, but only after gathering sufficient input so that the evaluative framework well fits the individual(s) with whom he or she is interacting. Asks questions, restates others' ideas, appears to gather information, prior to responding evaluatively.

Rating Scale

1   2   3   4   5

(Place "x" to indicate position on continuum)

17. Respect

Participant: _____

Rater: _____

Date: _____

Instructions:

There are different degrees to which individuals express respect or positive regard for other persons around them. These behaviors may take many forms ranging from verbal and non-verbal expressions of minimal interest and regard, to statements, gestures, and tones which are extremely supportive and demonstrate high regard and respect. For each individual please indicate on a 1 to 5 continuum, which pattern of expression was most characteristic during observation.

Description

1. The verbal and non-verbal expressions of the individual suggest a *clear lack of respect and negative regard* for others around him or her. By their actions the individual indicates that the feelings and experiences of others are not worthy of consideration or that others are not capable of acting constructively on their own. Examples include a condescending tone, lack of eye contact, general lack of interest, etc.
2. The individual responds to others in a way that communicates *little respect* for others' feelings, experiences, or potentials. The individual may respond mechanically or passively, or may appear to ignore many of the thoughts and feelings of others.
3. The individual indicates some respect for others' situations and *some concern* for their feelings, experiences, and potentials. The individual may indicate some attentiveness to others' efforts to express themselves.
4. The individual indicates a *concern* for the feelings, experiences, and potentials of others. The individual responds such as to enable others to feel worthy of interaction, and provides others a sense of being valued as individuals.
5. The individual indicates a *deep respect* for the worth of others as persons of high potential and worth. The individual indicates a clear and strong respect through eye contact, general attentiveness, appropriate tone, and general interest, demonstrates a clear respect for the thoughts and feelings of others, and seems committed to supporting and encouraging their development.

Rating Scale

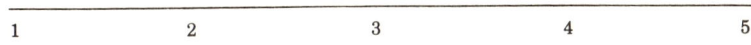

| 1 | 2 | 3 | 4 | 5 |

(Place "x" to indicate position on continuum)